Design and Implementation of Datacenter Protocols for Cloud Computing

Design and Implementation of Datacenter Protocols for Cloud Computing

Alex X Liu
Ant Financial, USA

Ali Munir
Cornell University, USA

World Scientific

NEW JERSEY · LONDON · SINGAPORE · BEIJING · SHANGHAI · HONG KONG · TAIPEI · CHENNAI · TOKYO

Published by

World Scientific Publishing Co. Pte. Ltd.

5 Toh Tuck Link, Singapore 596224

USA office: 27 Warren Street, Suite 401-402, Hackensack, NJ 07601

UK office: 57 Shelton Street, Covent Garden, London WC2H 9HE

British Library Cataloguing-in-Publication Data
A catalogue record for this book is available from the British Library.

DESIGN AND IMPLEMENTATION OF DATACENTER PROTOCOLS FOR CLOUD COMPUTING

ISBN 978-981-122-404-1 (hardcover)
ISBN 978-981-122-405-8 (ebook for institutions)
ISBN 978-981-122-406-5 (ebook for individuals)

For any available supplementary material, please visit
https://www.worldscientific.com/worldscibooks/10.1142/11931#t=suppl

Dedicated with love and respect
to my parents
Yuhai Liu (God rest his soul) and Shuxiang Wang,
to my wife
Chenyang Li,
to my twin sons
Max Boyang and Louis Boyang,
to whom I owe
all that I am and all that I have accomplished.

– Alex X. Liu

To my dearest parents, sisters and wife.

– Ali Munir

Preface

Datacenters have become a critical infrastructure for hosting user-facing online services such as web search, stock trading, social networking, and product advertising. Such services usually generate a large number of short but latency-sensitive flows and a small number of long but delay-tolerant flows. For short flows, even a fraction of a second increase in latency can make a quantifiable difference in application performance, which in turn, impacts user experience and operator revenue. With today's TCP that treats short and long flows equally, short flows suffer from high latency as long flows tend to occupy most of the buffer space in switches.

For datacenter transport, this book focuses on the design and implementation details of state-of-art transport protocols that not only achieves optimal performance in terms of minimizing flow completion times but are also deployment friendly. To this end, we first identified the underlying strategies used by existing datacenter transports. Next, we showed that these strategies are *complimentary* to each other, rather than *substitutes*, as they have different strengths and can address each other's limitations. Unfortunately, prior datacenter transports use only one of these strategies and as a result they either achieve near-optimal performance or deployment friendliness but not both. Based on this insight, we designed a datacenter transport protocol called PASE, which carefully synthesizes these strategies by assigning different transport responsibility to each strategy. PASE achieves both near-optimal performance as well as deployment friendliness. PASE does not require any changes in network switches (hardware or software); yet, it achieves comparable, or even better, performance than the state-of-the-art protocols (such as pFabric) that require changes to network elements.

To improve the performance of datacenter transport in multi-tenant networks, we proposed Stacked Congestion Control (SCC), to achieve performance isolation and objective scheduling simultaneously. SCC is a distributed host-based bandwidth allocation framework, where an underlay congestion control layer handles contention among tenants, and a private congestion control layer for each tenant optimizes its performance objective. SCC is designed based on the idea that, bandwidth allocation in datacenters should support not only performance isolation among tenants but also objective-oriented scheduling among flows from the same tenant. Moreover, bandwidth allocation design should be practical and readily-deployable.

For datacenter task placement, the book discusses the innovative framework called NEAT, that leverages information from the underlying network scheduler to make task placement decisions. To improve the performance of data-intensive applications, existing datacenter schedulers optimize either the placement of tasks or the scheduling of network flows. Inconsistent assumptions of the two schedulers can compromise the overall application performance. The core of NEAT is a task completion time predictor that estimates the completion time of a task under given network condition and a given network scheduling policy. Next, a distributed task placement framework leverages the predicted task completion times to make task placement decisions and minimize the average completion time of active tasks.

Contents

5. Bandwidth Allocation in Multi-tenant Datacenters   87

Chapter 1

Background and Motivation

Datacenters have become a critical infrastructure for hosting user-facing online services such as web search, stock trading, social networking, and product advertising. Such services usually generate a large number of short but latency-sensitive flows and a small number of long but delay-tolerant flows [Abts and Felderman (2012); Alizadeh *et al.* (2010, 2013a)]. For short flows, even a fraction of a second increase in latency can make a quantifiable difference in application performance, which in turn, impacts user experience and operator revenue. For example, Amazon found that every additional 100ms of latency costs them 1% loss in business revenue [Hong *et al.* (2012a)]. With today's TCP that treats short and long flows equally, short flows suffer from high latency as long flows tend to occupy most of the buffer space in switches [Alizadeh *et al.* (2010); Vamanan *et al.* (2012a)]. Thus, datacenter networks need a new transport protocol and task scheduling mechanisms that can minimize the latency for short flows yet achieve high throughput for long flows. Similarly, with today's task scheduling policies, network state is ignored while making task placement decisions. Therefore, there is a need for network state aware task placement framework.

1.1   A Near-Optimal Transport for Datacenters

Unfortunately, prior datacenter transport protocols either achieve near-optimal performance (in terms of minimizing flow completion times or maximizing the number of deadlines met) or deployment friendliness (i.e., require no changes in switch hardware) but not both. For example, protocols like PDQ [Hong *et al.* (2012a)] and pFabric [Alizadeh *et al.* (2013a)] can minimize average flow completion times (AFCTs) but require switches to perform complex operations that are not available in commercial switches and thus mandate modifications to switch hardware. On the other hand, protocols like DCTCP [Alizadeh *et al.* (2010)], L^{2}DCT [Munir *et al.* (2013b)], and D^{2}TCP [Vamanan *et al.* (2012a)] achieve deployment friendliness but lack global coordination between flows, which leads to sub-optimal flow scheduling. In this book, we ask: *how can we design a datacenter transport protocol that achieves both near-optimal flow scheduling as well as deployment friendliness?*

Towards this end, we first identify three underlying strategies used in prior datacenter transport protocols, namely *in-network prioritization* (used in pFabric [Alizadeh *et al.* (2013a)]), *arbitration* (used in D^3 [Wilson *et al.* (2011a)] and PDQ [Hong *et al.* (2012a)]), and *self-adjusting at endpoints* (used in DCTCP [Alizadeh *et al.* (2010)] and L^{2}DCT [Munir *et al.* (2013b)]). With in-network prioritization, switches schedule and drop packets based on the priority of each packet, thus allowing each switch to *locally* prioritize short flows over long flows. In the arbitration strategy, every network link has an arbitrator (implemented at a switch or a host) that allocates rates to each flow in real-time based on the global view of all active flows. With the self-adjusting at end-points strategy, each sender independently decides to increase or decrease their rate based on the observed congestion in the network.

Our key insight is that these three strategies, which were used individually before, are in fact complementary to each other and can be unified to work together nicely. For example, approaches that rely on arbitration alone have high flow switching overhead because flows need to be explicitly paused and unpaused. With in-network prioritization using strict priority queues inside switches, switching from a high priority flow to the next is seamless. Conversely, in-network prioritization approaches typically need to support a large number of priority levels whereas existing switches only have a limited number of priority queues. Arbitration addresses this problem by dynamically changing the mapping of flows to queues. Flows whose turn is far away are all mapped to the lowest priority queue while flows whose turn is about to come are mapped to the high priority queues.

Based on the above insights, we propose PASE; a transport protocol for datacenters that achieves near-optimal performance as well as deployment friendliness by synthesizing the three strategies, in-network <u>P</u>rioritization, <u>A</u>rbitration, and <u>S</u>elf-adjusting at <u>E</u>ndpoints. The design of PASE is based on the underlying principle that each strategy should focus on what it is best at doing. Arbitrators should do inter-flow prioritization at coarse timescales. They should not be responsible for computing precise rates or for doing fine-grained prioritization. End-points should react to congestion or spare capacity on their own, without involving any other entity. Further, given their lack of global information, they should not try to achieve inter-flow prioritization. We have observed that protocols that try to do this have poor performance. In-network prioritization mechanism should focus on per-packet prioritization at short, sub-RTT timescales.

This division of responsibilities among the three strategies follows the well-known *separation of concerns* principle and makes PASE perform comparable to the state-of-the-art transport protocols while also being deployment friendly, *i.e.*, requiring no changes to the network switches. A key aspect of PASE is a scalable control plane for arbitration. PASE uses distributed arbitrators that decide the priority of a flow given other flows in the system. For every link in the datacenter topology, PASE uses a dedicated arbitrator for arbitration. This functionality can be implemented at the endpoints themselves (e.g., for their own links to the switch) or on dedicated nodes within the datacenter. The outcome of arbitration is the priority queue and reference rate for a flow. At endpoints, PASE uses a TCP-like endpoint transport protocol, which leverages the priority queue and reference rate information for its rate control. At switches, PASE leverages *existing* priority queues to prioritize the scheduling of packets over network links.

To achieve its goals, the first challenge for PASE is to minimize the arbitration latency and arbitration overhead. Arbitration latency depends on the distance between the end-hosts and their corresponding arbitrators. This delay matters most during flow setup time as it can end up increasing the flow completion times, especially for short flows. Due to a separate control plane, each arbitration message is potentially processed as a separate packet by the switches which consumes their bandwidth and also require processing at arbitrators. We need to ensure that this overhead is kept low and that it does not cause network congestion for our primary traffic and does not add any significant processing delay.

To overcome these challenges, we exploit the typical tree-based datacenter topology features [Abts and Felderman (2012); Al-Fares *et al.* (2008)] to make the arbitration decisions in a bottom up fashion, starting from the end-points and going up to the root. This has several performance and scalability benefits. First, for intra-rack communication, which constitutes a sizeable share of datacenter traffic [Alizadeh *et al.* (2010)], only the source and destination are involved, obviating the need to communicate with any other entity. Second, lower level arbitrators (those closer to the leaf nodes) can do early pruning by discarding those flows that are unlikely to become part of the top priority queue. Third, high level arbitrators (those closer to the root) can *delegate* their arbitration decision to lower level arbitrators. Both early pruning and delegation reduce the arbitration latency and arbitration overhead, of course, at the cost of potentially less accurate decisions. PASE evaluation shows that these optimizations improve performance by up to 10% and reduce arbitration overhead by up to 60%.

Loss recovery in PASE is more challenging because packets can be delayed in a lower priority queue, which may trigger spurious timeouts, if we use today's timeout mechanisms. Thus, for lower priority flows, instead of retransmitting the data packet, PASE uses small *probe* packets that help in determining whether the packet was lost or was delayed.

We evaluate PASE using a small testbed and ns2 [ns2 (2006)] simulations. In terms of flow completion times, compared to deployment friendly protocols, PASE improves the average FCT (AFCT) by 40% to 60% for various scenarios; compared to near-optimal protocols, PASE performs within 6% of pFabric in scenarios where pFabric is close to optimal while in other scenarios, PASE outperforms pFabric by almost 80% both in terms of the AFCT and the 99th percentile FCT.

PASE shows the promise of combining existing transport strategies in a single transport framework. We view it as a first step towards a more holistic approach for building the next generation datacenter transport protocols.

1.2 Task Placement in Datacenters

Data transfer time has a significant impact on task completion times within a datacenter because most datacenter applications (such as MapReduce [Dean and Ghemawat (2008)], Pregel [Malewicz *et al.* (2010)], MPI [Gropp *et al.* (1998)], Dryad [Isard *et al.* (2007)]) are data-intensive and they need to access data that are distributed throughout the network. For example, for MapReduce, 30% task completion time is spent on transferring data across the network [Zaharia *et al.* (2010)]. For large commercial datacenters, the transfer of shuffle data is the dominant source of network traffic [Ahmad *et al.* (2014)]. In Facebook [Zaharia *et al.* (2010)] MapReduce clusters, 20% jobs are shuffle-heavy (i.e., generate a large amount of shuffle data), and in Yahoo! clusters [Chen *et al.* (2011)] this goes up to 60%. The network congestion caused by shuffle data is a key factor that degrades the performance of MapReduce jobs [Costa *et al.* (2012)]. Therefore, data transfer time in datacenter is critical for improving application performance.

Prior work on minimizing data transfer time falls into two categories: task placement ([Zaharia *et al.* (2010); Ahmad *et al.* (2014); Isard *et al.* (2009); Ananthanarayanan *et al.* (2010); Tan *et al.* (2014); Jalaparti *et al.* (2015)]) and network scheduling ([Hong *et al.* (2012b); Zats *et al.* (2012a); Munir *et al.* (2013c); Alizadeh *et al.* (2013b); Munir *et al.* (2014); Bai *et al.* (2015); Chowdhury and Stoica (2012); Dogar *et al.* (2014a); Chowdhury *et al.* (2014); Zhao *et al.* (2015); Chowdhury and Stoica (2015)]). The idea of task placement is to place compute tasks close to input data so that data locality is maximized and network traffic is minimized [Zaharia *et al.* (2010); Isard *et al.* (2009); Ananthanarayanan *et al.* (2010)]. The idea of network scheduling is to schedule the flows or groups of flows (i.e., coflows) generated by tasks, at shared links, based on given flow properties (such as size, deadline, and correlation among flows) and given task placement to minimize flow completion times[Hong *et al.* (2012b); Munir *et al.* (2013c); Alizadeh *et al.* (2013b); Munir *et al.* (2014); Chowdhury *et al.* (2014)]. The limitation of prior task placement policies is that they design traffic matrix assuming fair sharing of network bandwidth and ignore the priorities assigned to different flows by the network scheduler; meanwhile, network schedulers schedule flows based on flow priorities (such as size or deadline) and the flow completion time of a low priority flow can increase if placed on a path sharing links with high priority flows. The limitation of network schedulers is that the source/destination of each flow is independently decided by the task schedulers and not necessarily optimal.

We propose NEAT, a **N**etwork-sch**E**duling-**A**ware **T**ask placement framework that leverages *network scheduling policy* and *network state* in making task placement decisions for data-intensive applications. The placement by NEAT coupled with a properly selected network scheduling policy ensures that tasks are finished as quickly as possible. The intuition behind NEAT is that a good placement of data-intensive tasks should spread the flows to minimize the sharing of network links. When sharing is inevitable, however, the preferred placement strategy depends on how the network schedules flows, as illustrated by the following example.

Let us consider a simple scenario in Figure 1.1, where we want to place a task R that needs to read data from task M running on node 2 onto candidate hosts node 1 or node 3. At the current time, the network has one flow with remaining size of $4\,\mathrm{Gb}$ on path $2 \to 3$ and requires four more

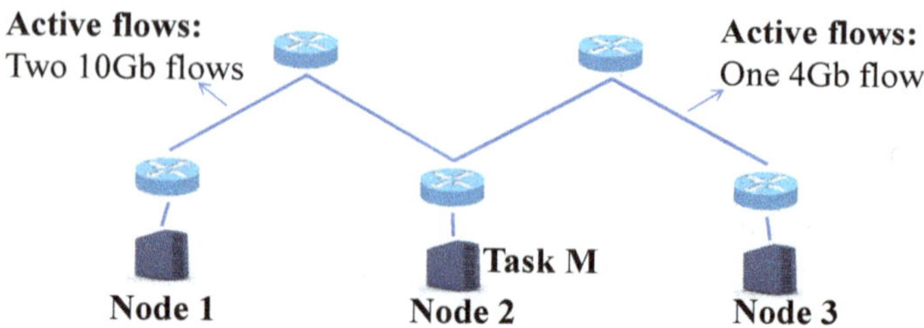

Candidate hosts: Node 1 or 3,　**New Flow (R) size**: 5 Gb,
Link capacity: 1 Gbps

Network Scheduling Policy	Placement of R	Completion time of R (s)	Increase in Total Completion time (s)
FCFS	Node 1	25	25
	Node 3	**9**	**9**
Fair	Node 1	15	25
	Node 3	**9**	**13**
SRPT	**Node 1**	**5**	**15**
	Node 3	9	9

Fig. 1.1　Network scheduling aware placement.

seconds (on 1 Gbps link) to finish if running alone. There are two other flows on path $2 \to 1$, each of remaining size 10 Gb, thus requiring ten more seconds if running alone. Suppose that the input data of candidate task R is of size 5 Gb and our goal is to finish the task as quickly as possible. Assuming First Come First Serve scheduling (FCFS) in the network, we will place task R on node 3, as it provides the smaller completion time of 9 seconds as compared to 25 seconds when placed on node 1, because flow R will not be scheduled until the existing flows finish data transfer. Assuming fair scheduling (Fair) in the network, we will place task R on node 3, as it requires 9 seconds to complete flow R on node 3 compared to 15 seconds on node 1. Assuming the network uses shortest remaining processing time (SRPT) scheduling, we will place task R on node 1, as it can finish in 5 seconds on node 1 by preempting both the existing flows. We assume flows with the same priority share the network fairly as in existing solutions [Alizadeh *et al.* (2013b); Munir *et al.* (2014)]. However, if the goal is to minimize the increase in total (i.e., sum) flow completion time of all the active flows in the network, then under SRPT, the scheduler will choose node 3 to minimize the increase in completion time of flows in the network (i.e., completion time of new flow plus increased completion times of existing flows). We see that the optimal task placement in a network can vary depending on the network scheduling policy and the network performance metric.

NEAT leverages these insights in its design and provides a task placement framework to minimize the average flow completion time (AFCT) in the network. NEAT employs a task performance predictor that predicts the completion time of a given task under an arbitrary network scheduling policy. NEAT is quite pluggable in terms of better resource or application models and predictors. NEAT makes task placement decision in two steps: first, it predicts task performance by hypothetically placing a task on each candidate node and analyzing its performance based on the network scheduling policy and the network state. Next, it selects a node for the task based on the predicted task completion time and a node state, that characterizes the sizes of existing flows. The proposed task placement mechanism focuses on network performance in task placement decisions and only uses node properties (e.g., CPU, memory) to determine whether a node is a candidate host. We leave joint placement to future work. To realize this idea, NEAT addresses two challenges:

The first technical challenge in designing NEAT is to *accurately predict the performance of a task for a given network state and scheduling policy.* We use the completion time of data transfer, i.e., the *flow completion time (FCT)* or the *coflow completion time (CCT),* to measure the overall task performance. Compared to network-centric performance metrics such as delay, jitter, and available bandwidth, completion time is task-centric and better models network conditions in terms of their impact on task performance (§4.6).

The second technical challenge is to *efficiently collect network state information and make placement decisions.* As illustrated in Figure 1.2, NEAT uses a distributed control framework with two components: a local controller (network daemon) that maintains a *compressed* state of all active flows (or coflows) on each node to predict task completion times, and a global controller (task placement daemon) that gathers the predicted task completion times from local controllers to make task placement decisions. Here, a "node" refers to an endhost (e.g., server) capable of running tasks. Using the flow state information, the local controllers predict the FCT/CCT on edge links (i.e., links directly connected to nodes), based on which the global controller uses a greedy algorithm to pick the node whose edge link has the smallest FCT/CCT. To reduce communications with the

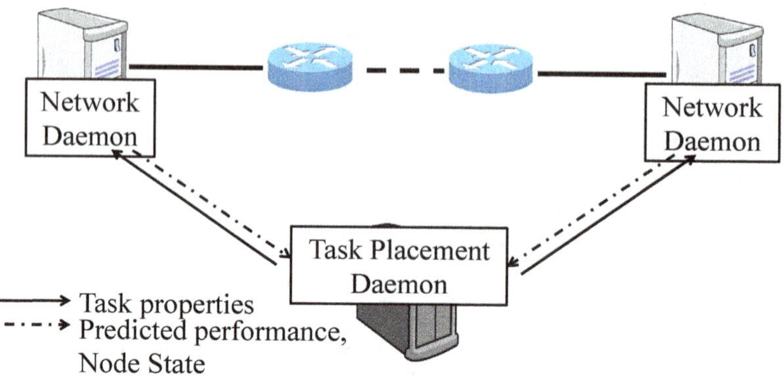

Fig. 1.2   NEAT Architecture.

local controllers, the global controller also maintains a *state* for each node, defined as the remaining size of the smallest active flow on that node, such that only nodes with preferred states (no less than the size of the current flow) are contacted.

NEAT does not require any changes to the network. However, it requires task information (e.g., size) from applications, similar to prior works [Alizadeh *et al.* (2013b); Munir *et al.* (2014); Chowdhury and Stoica (2012)], to accurately predict task completion time. For recurrent workloads, this information can be inferred by monitoring task execution [Jalaparti *et al.* (2015)].

NEAT's performance is upper-bounded by the underlying network (flow/coflow) scheduling policy. When the network scheduling policy is suboptimal (e.g., Fair, LAS), when our goal is FCT, there is plenty of room for improvement and NEAT is able to significantly improve the task performance; when the network scheduling policy is near optimal (SRPT), the room for improvement is reduced, NEAT still achieves notable improvement for such scenarios.

We evaluate NEAT using both a trace-driven simulator and a 10-machine testbed based on a variety of production workloads [Dean and Ghemawat (2008); Alizadeh *et al.* (2013b)] and network scheduling policies such as DCTCP [Alizadeh *et al.* (2011)], L^{2}DCT [Munir *et al.* (2013c)], PASE [Munir *et al.* (2014)], and Varys [Chowdhury *et al.* (2014)]. We evaluate two other state-of-art task placement policies: *minLoad* that always selects a node with the minimum load, measured by the total size of flows scheduled on that node, and *minDist* that always selects a node closest to the input data. NEAT performs 3.7x better than alternative strategies when the underlying network scheduling policy is Fair (DCTCP [Alizadeh *et al.* (2011)]), 3x better when the policy is least attained service (LAS) (L²DCT [Munir *et al.* (2013c)]), and 30% better when the policy is SRPT (PASE [Munir *et al.* (2014)]). In both cases, NEAT improves performance by being aware of the network scheduling policy. In particular, since Fair is the underlying policy in most commercial datacenters, NEAT can significantly improve the performance of data-intensive applications in majority of cases.

1.3   Bandwidth Allocation in Multi-tenant Datacenters

In datacenter networks, flows can have different performance objectives. A private datacenter is shared by various tenants, such as search engine, advertising and e-Business applications. Each tenant can run many service entities (*e.g.*, Virtual Machines, Containers, Java processes) that communicate over the underlying network. The flows generated by these services have different performance objectives due to their service requirements. Some flows are *Latency-Sensitive (LS)*: service can enqueue copies of a task in multiple servers to combat computation time variability [Dean and Barroso (2013)]; to minimize resource wastage, a cancelation message should be sent to the counterpart servers as soon as the first replica is finished. On the other hand, some flows are *Deadline-Sensitive (DS)*: the partition-aggregate architecture of Online Data Intensive applications (OLDI) [Jalaparti *et al.* (2013); DeCandia *et al.* (2007)] and real-time analytic [Melnik *et al.* (2010); Engle *et al.* (2012)] enforce deadline semantics for every leaf-to-parent flow. Furthermore for many other applications, minimizing average flow-completion-time (AFCT) can significantly improve their performance [Alizadeh *et al.* (2013b); Hong *et al.* (2012b); Munir *et al.* (2014)], and we call these flows as *Completion-Sensitive (CS)* flows. We use a *tenant-objective division* to denote all the flows of a tenant that share the same performance objective.

Bandwidth allocation in datacenters should support not only performance isolation among divisions but also objective-oriented scheduling among flows within the same division. Bandwidth allocation design, in essence, defines how flows behave when congestion happens. Most datacenter networks are oversubscribed [Farrington and Andreyev (2013)] and congestion is not uncommon: packet drops due to congestion can be observed when the whole network utilization is around only 25% [Singh *et al.* (2015)]. To achieve performance isolation, administrators can assign weights to different divisions that share the underlying network [Shieh *et al.* (2011)]. For example, upon congestion, an administrator may prefer tenant A's DS flows over tenant B's DS flows, or all tenants' LS flows over their CS flows. Various techniques can be used to support objective-oriented flow scheduling: some reduce tail latency of messages [Alizadeh *et al.* (2011, 2012); Jang *et al.* (2015); Grosvenor *et al.* (2015)], some add deadline awareness [Hong *et al.* (2012b); Wilson *et al.* (2011b); Vamanan *et al.* (2012b); Zhang *et al.* (2015)], and others focus on reducing AFCT [Hong *et al.* (2012b); Zats *et al.* (2012a); Munir *et al.* (2013c); Alizadeh *et al.* (2013b); Munir *et al.* (2014); Perry *et al.* (2014); Bai *et al.* (2015); Mittal *et al.* (2015); Gao *et al.* (2015)].

Many of the existing objective-oriented approaches [Hong *et al.* (2012b); Alizadeh *et al.* (2011, 2012); Jang *et al.* (2015); Grosvenor *et al.* (2015); Zats *et al.* (2012a); Munir *et al.* (2013c); Alizadeh *et al.* (2013b); Munir *et al.* (2014); Perry *et al.* (2014); Bai *et al.* (2015); Mittal *et al.* (2015); Gao *et al.* (2015)] are designed to achieve only a single performance objective at a time, and there could be severe interference if approaches of different objectives coexist without isolation. This happens because these approaches may detect congestion differently (*e.g.*, packet drop, or ECN) or react to congestion differently (*e.g.*, the ECN co-existence problem in production Cloud [Sivaraman *et al.* (2013); Judd (2015)]). pFabric [Alizadeh *et al.* (2013b)] and Karuna [Chen *et al.* (2016)] evaluate the coexistence of the DS and CS flows by setting absolute priority to DS flows over CS flows. However, performance isolation among flows with the same objective but of different tenants is not considered. Furthermore, existing performance isolation approaches cannot optimize performance objectives for individual tenant-objective division. Neither bandwidth guarantee [Guo *et al.* (2010); Rodrigues *et al.* (2011); Jeyakumar *et al.* (2013a); Popa *et al.* (2013); Lee *et al.* (2014); Hu *et al.* (2016)] nor proportional sharing [Shieh *et al.* (2011)] can perform bandwidth allocation at flow-level granularity.

Bandwidth allocation design should be practical and readily-deployable. Many works either require non-trivial switch modifications [Alizadeh *et al.* (2012); Hong *et al.* (2012b); Zats *et al.* (2012a); Alizadeh *et al.* (2013b); Dogar *et al.* (2014a)], or assume non-blocking network, which is not widely available in production datacenter [Gao *et al.* (2015)]. A centralized scheduling mechanism (*e.g.*, Fastpass [Perry *et al.* (2014)]) may perform optimization for all divisions, but requires an ideally scalable control plane and time synchronization for arbitration.

In this book, we discuss our proposed Stacked Congestion Control (SCC), a distributed host-based bandwidth allocation framework. SCC can support both *performance isolation* and *objective scheduling*, and is readily-deployable. SCC has two layers to perform congestion control: (i) an underlay congestion control (UCC) layer handles contention among divisions (*i.e.* performance isolation), and (ii) a private congestion control (PCC) layer for each division to optimize its performance objective (*i.e.* objective scheduling). UCC supports the following abstraction: a weight (obtained via administrator policy or utility function maximization [Popa *et al.* (2012)]) is attached with each division; each division should get a bandwidth share that is proportional to its weight.

The first challenge is how to achieve weighted bandwidth allocation by controlling the active flows within each division in a distributed and transparent way. Irrespective of the tenant-objective division semantic, TCP (and its variants) only allocates bandwidth proportional to the contending flows. SCC thus introduces *tenant-objective tunnel* as an edge-based abstraction (between every eligible pair of source and destination hosts, flows of each division are aggregated inside a dedicated point-to-point tunnel). Each tunnel is assigned a weight (dynamically updated by the division's PCC) and SCC allocates the bandwidth share to a tunnel in proportion to its weight. Because of the state-of-the-art multi-path load balancing schemes (*e.g.*, Presto [He *et al.* (2015)]) in datacenter (*e.g.*, Clos-network), the share of a tunnel in each network tier is statistically proportional to its weight. Our key insight is that the division's bandwidth share can be achieved by cooperatively scaling each tunnel's network weight if the tunnels in the same division ensure that the sum of their weights equals the global weight of the division.

The second challenge is how to support two congestion control mechanisms (UCC and PCC) simultaneously. For distributed host-based bandwidth allocation, two factors define congestion control behaviour: (i) *congestion signal*, i.e., what method is used to detect network congestion, and (ii) *control law*, i.e., what rate increase (decrease) law is used to grab (yield) network bandwidth. The dilemma is that, to respect performance isolation, all tunnels should follow the same UCC mechanism; there is only one uniform set of congestion signal available from the network, which reflects the contention among tunnels; it cannot be directly exploited for objective-oriented congestion control inside each tunnel. Our technical contribution here is to add a rate-limiting queue in the ingress of each tunnel to completely decouple two congestion control mechanisms. UCC uses ECN as the congestion signal and uses weighted network sharing algorithms (similar to Seawall [Shieh *et al.* (2011)]) to derive the tunnel rate according to network condition. Moreover, each sender queue can locally generate desired congestion signal for PCC layer.

Further, we develop PCC algorithms for every objective to dynamically derive the per-tunnel weight, so that each tunnel is allocated a weight according to the demand of its flows as compared to other flows within the same division. Besides existing objective-oriented scheduling approaches, we also develop new in-tunnel scheduling algorithms to exploit the extra flexibility provided by SCC.

We implement SCC as a Linux kernel module using NetFilter. We evaluate SCC on a small-scale testbed with 16 Dell servers and a commodity PICA-8 Gigabit Ethernet switch with ECN enabled. To complement our small-scale testbed experiments, we further conduct large-scale simulations using NS-2. SCC can meet requirements of performance objectives, when flows of different objectives coexist in the datacenter networks. Compared to the direct coexistence cases, SCC reduces latency by up to 40% for Latency-Sensitive flows, deadline miss ratio by up to 3.2× for Deadline-Sensitive flows, and average flow-completion-time by up to 53% for Completion-Sensitive flows.

Chapter 2

Overview of Prior Solutions

In this chapter, the overview and limitations of existing approaches using some case studies is discussed.

2.1 A Near-Optimal Transport for Datacenters

2.1.1 *Related Work*

We can categorize prior works in terms of the underlying transport strategies they use.

Self-Adjusting Endpoints: Several data center transports use this strategy [Alizadeh *et al.* (2010); Munir *et al.* (2013b); Vamanan *et al.* (2012a); Chen *et al.* (2013)]. DCTCP uses an adaptive congestion control mechanism based on ECN to maintain low queues. D^2TCP and L^2DCT add deadline-awareness and size-awareness to DCTCP, respectively. MCP [Chen *et al.* (2013)] improves performance over D^2TCP by assigning more precise flow rates using ECN marks. These rates are based on the solution of a stochastic delay minimization problem. These protocols do not support flow preemption and in-network prioritization, which limits their performance.

Arbitration: PDQ [Hong *et al.* (2012a)] and D^3 [Wilson *et al.* (2011a)] use network-wide arbitration but incur high flow switching overhead. PASE's bottom up approach to arbitration has similarities with EyeQ [Jeyakumar *et al.* (2013b)], which targets a different problem of providing bandwidth guarantees in multi-tenant cloud data centers. PASE's arbitration mechanism generalizes EyeQ's arbitration by dealing with scenarios where contention can occur at links other than the access links.

In-network Prioritization: pFabric [Alizadeh *et al.* (2013a)] uses in-network prioritization by doing priority-based scheduling/dropping of packets. DeTail [Zats *et al.* (2012b)], a cross layer network stack, focuses on minimizing the *tail* latency but does not target the average FCT. In [Kumar *et al.* (2013)], authors propose virtual shapers to overcome the challenge of limited number of rate limiters. While both DeTail and virtual shapers use in-network prioritization, they do not provide mechanisms for achieving network-wide arbitration.

In general, prior proposals target one specific transport strategy, PASE uses all these strategies in unison to overcome limitations of individual strategies and thus achieves high performance across a wide range of scenarios while being deployment friendly.

To achieve high performance, which means to minimize completion times, maximize throughput, or reduce the deadline miss rate [Alizadeh *et al.* (2010, 2013a); Hong *et al.* (2012a)], existing datacenter transports use one or two of the following three transport strategies: (1) *self-adjusting at endpoints*, (2) *arbitration*, or (3) *in-network prioritization*. In this section, we first introduce these strategies and discuss their limitations when they are employed in isolation. Then, we discuss how these limitations can be addressed if these strategies are used together.

2.1.2   *Limitations of using Transport Strategies in Isolation*

Each transport strategy has its own strengths and limitations as shown in Table 2.1. We now introduce the basic working of each strategy, discuss its strengths, and validate their limitations through simulation experiments.

Self-Adjusting at Endpoints: With this strategy, endpoints themselves decide the amount of data to send based on network congestion status, which is determined through congestion signals that could be implicit (such as packet loss) or explicit (such as ECN). In case of congestion, if fairness is the objective, the window size is reduced by the same factor for all flows; if flow prioritization is the objective, the window size is reduced based on other parameters (such as the remaining flow size [Alizadeh *et al.* (2013a); Munir *et al.* (2013b)] or deadline [Vamanan *et al.* (2012a)]).

Protocols in this category are easy to deploy because they do not require any changes to the network infrastructure. However, when considering flow prioritization, their performance is inferior to the state-of-the-art datacenter transport protocols (such as pFabric [Alizadeh *et al.* (2013a)] and PDQ [Hong *et al.* (2012a)]) as they do not provide strict priority scheduling: even low priority flows, which should be paused, continue to send at least one packet per RTT. Thus, this hurts transport performance, especially at high

Transport Strategy	Pros	Cons
Self-Adjusting Endpoints	Ease of deployment	Lack of support for strict priority scheduling
Arbitration	(1) Support for strict priority scheduling (2) Fast convergence to allocated rates	(1) High flow switching overhead (2) Hard to compute precise flow rates
In-network Prioritization	(1) Work conservation (2) Low flow switching overhead	(1) Limited number of priority queues in switches (2) Switch-local decisions lead to sub-optimal performance

loads when multiple flows are simultaneously active.

To demonstrate this behavior, we take two protocols that follow the self-adjusting end-point strategy, DCTCP [Alizadeh *et al.* (2010)] and D^{2}TCP [Vamanan *et al.* (2012a)] (a deadline-aware version of DCTCP), and compare their performance with pFabric [Alizadeh *et al.* (2013a)], the state-of-the-art datacenter transport with the best reported performance. We replicate a deadline oriented scenario in ns2. This corresponds to the experiment section 4.1.3 in the D^{2}TCP [Vamanan *et al.* (2012a)]: it represents an intra-rack scenario, where the source and destination of each flow is picked randomly and the flow sizes are uniformly distributed between [100 KB, 500 KB] in the presence of two background long flows. The deadlines are uniformly distributed from 5 ms-25 ms. Figure 2.1(a) shows the fraction of deadlines met (or *application throughput*) as a function of load for the three schemes. While at low loads, D^{2}TCP is able to meet deadlines (*i.e.*, achieve prioritization), at higher loads its performance approaches its fair-sharing counterpart, DCTCP. Moreover, both these protocols perform much worse than pFabric at high loads, highlighting their limitations in achieving priority scheduling across a wide range of network loads.

Arbitration: Explicit rate protocols, like PDQ [Hong *et al.* (2012a)], use this transport strategy. Instead of end-points making decisions on their own, arbitration based approaches [Hong *et al.* (2012a); Wilson *et al.* (2011a)] require the switches to make the scheduling decision, keeping in view all network flows and their individual priorities (e.g., deadline, flow size). The scheduling decision is communicated as a *rate* at which flows should send data at. The rate could be zero, if the flow needs to be paused because of its low priority, or it could be the full link capacity, if the flow has the highest priority. While a centralized problem in general, prior work [Hong *et al.* (2012a); Wilson *et al.* (2011a)] shows that arbitration

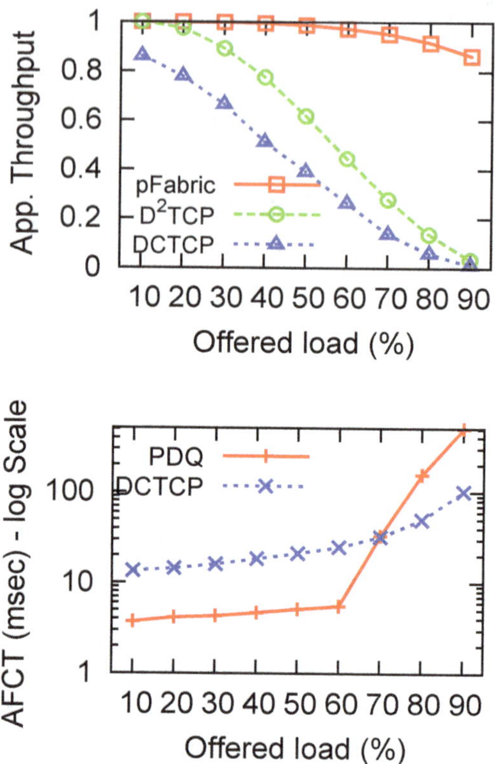

Fig. 2.1   Comparison of a) D^2TCP, DCTCP and pFabric, b) PDQ (an arbitration based approach) with DCTCP.

can be done in a decentralized fashion–each switch along the path of a flow adds its rate to the packet header and the minimum rate is picked by the sender for transmitting data.

The explicit nature of arbitration based approaches ensures that flows achieve their desired rate quickly (typically in one RTT). Moreover, the ability to pause and unpause flows enables strict priority scheduling of flows: highest priority flow gets the full link capacity (if it can saturate the link) while other flows are paused. However, the explicit rate assignment comes with its own set of problems. For example, calculating accurate rates for flows is challenging as flows could be bottlenecked at other non-network resources (e.g., source application, receiver, etc). Another important issue is the *flow switching overhead*, which refers to the overhead of pausing and unpausing flows. This overhead is typically around 1-2 RTTs, which can be significant in scenarios involving short flows (when flows last for a small duration) and at high network load (when flows need to be frequently preempted).

We illustrate the impact of flow switching overhead in a practical scenario through a simulation experiment. We consider PDQ [Hong *et al.* (2012a)][1], which is considered as the best performing arbitration based scheme, and compare its performance with DCTCP [Alizadeh *et al.* (2010)]. The scenario is a repeat of the previous intra-rack, all-to-all experiment, except the metric here is flow completion time. Figure 2.1(b) shows the average flow completion time as a function of network load. At low loads, PDQ outperforms DCTCP because of its fast convergence to the desired rate. However, at high loads, the flow switching overhead becomes significant as more flows contend with each other, thereby requiring more preemptions in the network. As a result, PDQ's performance degrades and the completion time becomes even higher than that of DCTCP.

In-network Prioritization: In transport protocols that use in-network prioritization (e.g., pFabric [Alizadeh *et al.* (2013a)]), packets carry flow priorities, such as the flow deadline or size, and the switches use this priority to decide which packet to schedule or drop (in case of congestion). This behavior ensures two desirable properties: *work conservation*, so a lower priority packet is scheduled if there is no packet belonging to the high priority, and *preemption*, which ensures that when a higher priority packet arrives, it gets precedence over a lower priority packet.

The well known downside to in-network prioritization is the limited number of priority queues available in switches–typically on the order of 8-12 [Wilson *et al.* (2011a)] (also see Table 3.1). For most practical scenarios, this number is much smaller than the number of unique flow priorities in the system. Proposals that can support larger number of *priority levels* require changing the network fabric [Alizadeh *et al.* (2013a)], which makes them hard to deploy.

Another shortcoming of this strategy is that switches make local decisions about prioritization which can lead to sub-optimal performance in multi-link scenarios. This is shown in Figure 2.2 through a simple toy example involving three flows. Flow 1 has the highest priority; Flow 2 has medium priority and flow 3 has the lowest priority. Flows 1 and 2 share link B, so only flow 1 can progress while flow 2 should wait. A protocol like pFabric continues to send packets of flow 2 on link A even though these

---

[1]Based on the simulator code obtained from the PDQ authors. It supports all the optimizations that reduce the flow switching overhead.

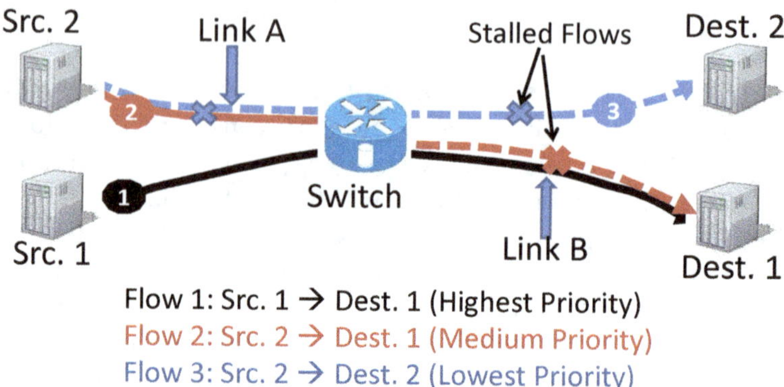

Fig. 2.2   Toy example illustrating problem with pFabric.

packets are dropped at link B. These unnecessary transmissions stall flow 3, which could have run in parallel with flow 1 as both flows do not share any link.

The above toy example highlights a common use case present in all-to-all traffic patterns (e.g., MapReduce [Dean and Ghemawat (2004)], Search) where a node typically has data to send to many other nodes. To quantify this problem under such practical settings, we simulate the interaction between workers and aggregators within a single rack of a search application. Each worker-aggregator flow is uniformly distributed between [2,198] KB. We focus on the loss rate of pFabric when the network load is increased. Figure 2.3 shows that loss rate shoots up as the load on network links is increased. For a load of 80%, more than 40% packets are dropped. These lost packets translate into throughput loss as we could have used these transmissions for packets belonging to other flows. Section 4.6 shows how this high loss rate results in poor flow completion time for pFabric.

2.1.3   *Motivation of using Transport Strategies in Unison*

We now discuss how *combining* these transport strategies offers a simple solution to the problems identified earlier.

In-network Prioritization complementing arbitration: The high flow switching overhead of arbitration-only approaches can be avoided with the help of in-network prioritization. As today's arbitration-only ap-

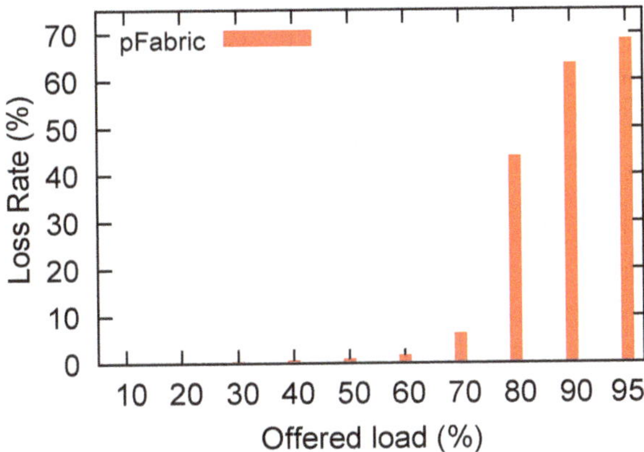

Fig. 2.3   Loss rate for pFabric as a function of load.

proaches, like PDQ [Hong *et al.* (2012a)], assume no prioritization within the network, they achieve priority scheduling by communicating explicit rates to end-hosts, which takes time, and thus results in a high flow switching overhead. If we have in-network prioritization, the arbitrator can just assign *relative* priorities to the flows (e.g., high priority flow vs. low priority flow), leaving it up to the switches to *enforce* this relative priority through a suitable scheduling and dropping mechanism. The current in-network prioritization mechanisms (e.g., priority queues) provide seamless switching between flows of different priorities, so there is no flow switching overhead and link utilization remains high during this period.

A simple example illustrates this benefit. Assume we have two flows–F_1 (higher priority) and F_2 (lower priority). With arbitration-only approaches, F_1 is initially assigned the entire link capacity while F_2 is paused during this time. When F_1 finishes, we have to explicitly signal F_2 to unpause. With in-network prioritization, we can just assign these flows to different priority classes–F_1 is mapped to the high priority class while F_2 is mapped to the low priority class. The switch ensures that as soon as there are no more packets of F_1 in the high priority queue, it starts scheduling packets of F_2 from the lower priority queue.

Arbitration aiding In-network Prioritization: The small number of priority queues cause performance degradation when multiple flows get mapped to the high priority queue [Alizadeh *et al.* (2013a)]. This results in multiplexing of these flows instead of strict priority scheduling (i.e., one flow at a time). This problem can be avoided with the help of arbitration. Instead of statically mapping flows to queues, an arbitrator can do a *dynamic* mapping. So a flow's priority queue keeps on changing during the flow's lifetime. Flows whose "turn" is far away are mapped to lower priority queues. As a flow's turn is about to come, it moves up to a higher priority queue.

We explain this idea through a simple two queue example. Suppose queue A (Q_A) is the high priority queue and queue B (Q_B) is the lower priority queue. We have four flows to schedule (F_1, F_2, F_3, and F_4, with F_1 having the highest priority and F_4, the lowest)–as the number of flows is more than the number of queues, any static mapping of flows to queues will result in sub-optimal performance. With the help of arbitration, we can initially map F_1 to Q_A and the other three flows to Q_B. When F_1 finishes, we can change the mapping of F_2 from Q_B to Q_A while flows F_3 and F_4 are still mapped to Q_B. Similar process is applied when F_2 (and later on, F_3) finishes. In short, the highest priority queue is used for the active, high priority flow while the lower priority queue is used primarily to keep link utilization high (i.e., work-conservation). The example shows how arbitration can help leverage the limited number of priority queues without compromising on performance.

Arbitration helping Self-Adjusting Endpoints: With arbitration-only approaches, calculating precise flow rates can be hard as the arbitrator may not have accurate information about all the possible bottlenecks in the system [Hong *et al.* (2012a); Wilson *et al.* (2011a)]. Thus, we can end up underestimating or overestimating the available capacity. Unfortunately, in arbitration-only approaches, end-points–which typically have a better idea of path conditions–are dumb: they always transmit at the rate assigned by the arbitrator, so even if they are in a position to detect congestion or spare capacity in the network, they cannot respond.

The self-adjusting end-point strategy naturally addresses this problem as it constantly probes the network: if there is any spare capacity, it will increase its rate, and if there is congestion, it will back off. For example, suppose there are two flows in the system with different priorities. The higher priority flow is assigned the full link capacity but it is unable to use it. The lower priority flow will remain paused if we do not use self-adjusting end-points. However, if the end-point uses a self-adjusting policy, it will detect spare capacity and increase its rate until the link is saturated. Note that arbitration also helps the self-adjusting end-point strategy: instead of just blindly probing the network for its due share, a flow can use information from the arbitrator to "bootstrap" the self-adjusting behavior.

2.2 Task Placement in Datacenters

2.2.1 *Related Work: Task Placement in Datacenters*

The related work can be divided in two categories: Task placement (or scheduling) and network scheduling.

Task Scheduling: State-of-art task schedulers follow the principle of "maximizing data locality" to minimize data transfer over the network. For the first stage of jobs (e.g., Map), techniques such as delay scheduling [Zaharia *et al.* (2010)] and flow-based scheduling [Isard *et al.* (2009)] try to place tasks on the machines or racks where most of their input data are located. Mantri instead optimizes the data locality while placing reducers [Ananthanarayanan *et al.* (2010)]. However, when the data is spread throughout the cluster (e.g., in distributed file systems like HDFS [Borthakur (2007)]), the subsequent job stages (e.g., shuffle phase) have to read data using cross-rack links, and often suffer from heavy network congestion [Chowdhury *et al.* (2013)]. To alleviate the problem, techniques like ShuffleWatcher [Ahmad *et al.* (2014)] attempt to localize the Map tasks of a job to one or a few racks, and thus reduce cross-rack shuffling. However, such techniques end up increasing the cross-rack transfer of the input data. A similar idea was exploited in Sinbad [Chowdhury *et al.* (2013)] to place the endpoints of flows to avoid congested links, but Sinbad is for a special type of flows (replicated file system writes) and is agnostic to the underlying network scheduling policy. When the input data of a job is known beforehand, techniques like Corral [Jalaparti *et al.* (2015)] can be used to pack the input data to a few racks such that all computation can be performed on local data. Similarly, many fairness based cluster scheduling frameworks [Ghodsi *et al.* (2011); Hindman *et al.* (2011); Ghodsi *et al.* (2012, 2013); Vavilapalli *et al.* (2013)] or straggler mitigation techniques [Zaharia *et al.* (2008); Ananthanarayanan *et al.* (2010, 2013); Ren *et al.* (2015)] have been proposed. However, these works assume fair sharing in the network and does not consider effect of underlying network scheduling policies. Another category of works [Chang *et al.* (2011); Chen *et al.* (2012)] does joint network and task execution scheduling, however these works assume that they have knowledge about task arrival times and make offline task scheduling decisions.

Network Scheduling: Generally, data-intensive jobs spend a substantial fraction of their execution time on data transfer [Zaharia *et al.* (2010)], and consequently, their performance critically depends on the performance of network scheduling. In recent years, a variety of network scheduling systems such as DCTCP [Alizadeh *et al.* (2011)], L^{2}DCT [Munir *et al.* (2013c)], PASE [Munir *et al.* (2014)], Varys [Chowdhury *et al.* (2014)], and Baraat [Dogar *et al.* (2014a)] have been proposed. Many of these protocols provide near-optimal data transfer time, but the improvement to the overall task performance is limited as they do not optimize the placement of sources/destinations of the flows.

NEAT addresses these limitations in two ways: it places the destinations of flows (via task placement) while taking into account the underlying network scheduling policy to minimize the overall data transfer time, and it uses a performance predictor that captures network state and essence of the network scheduling policies.

2.2.2 *Why Task Palcement needs Scheduling Awareness?*

Task placement policies perform differently when used with different network scheduling policies. To illustrate this, we compare the performance of two task scheduling policies under two different network scheduling policies. For task scheduling policies, we consider: minimum-distance placement (minDist), which places each task to minimize its distance to the input data, and minimum-load placement (minLoad), which places each task on the server with the minimum traffic load. For network scheduling policy, we consider: DCTCP [Alizadeh *et al.* (2011)], which approximates the Fair sharing policy, and PASE [Munir *et al.* (2014)], which approximates the shortest remaining processing time (SRPT) policy in the network.

We simulate a topology of 160 machines, connected using a folded CLOS topology as in [Munir *et al.* (2014)]. We configure the links to have 200μsec RTT and 1 Gbps (edge) or 10 Gbps (core) bandwidth. We evaluate each combination of the above task/network scheduling policies under flow demands generated according to the data-mining workload [Alizadeh *et al.* (2013b)]. Figure 2.4(a) and Figure 2.4(b) show the ratio between the FCT of minDist and the FCT of minLoad for various flow sizes under the Fair, and SRPT network scheduling policy, respectively. A bar with coordinates (x, y) indicates that flows of sizes x have an FCT ratio of y, where y¡1 indicates that minDist outperforms minLoad and y¿1 indicates the opposite.

The results show that when the network follows SRPT policy (Figure 2.4(a)), minDist placement works better (ratio less than 1). In contrast,

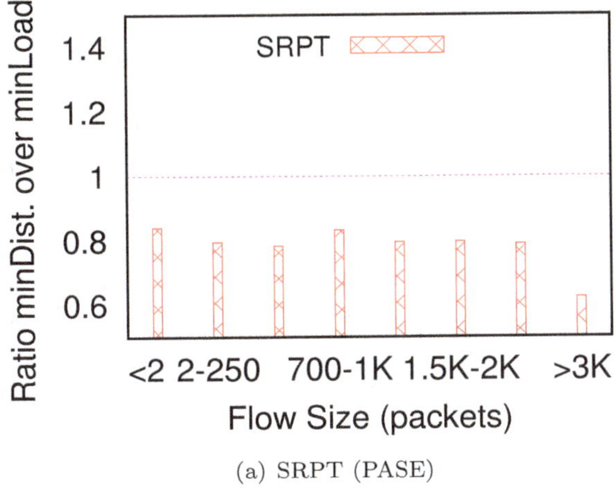

(a) SRPT (PASE)

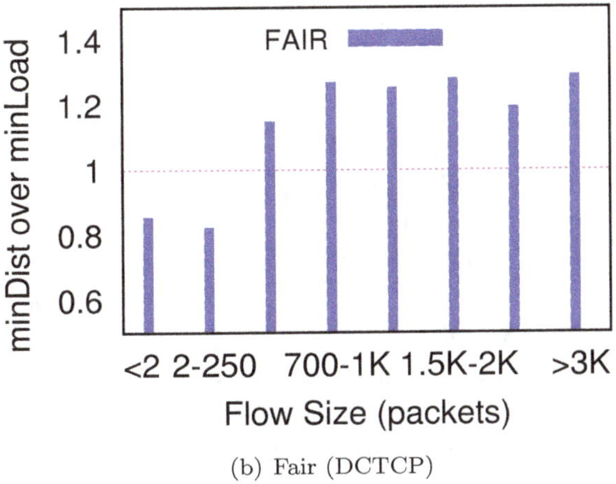

(b) Fair (DCTCP)

Fig. 2.4   Comparison of minDist and minLoad placement under SRPT and Fair network scheduling policy.

when the network follows a Fair policy (Figure 2.4(b)), minLoad placement works better for the majority of the flow sizes. The results can be explained by the following observations: when the network follows SRPT policy (Figure 2.4(a)), short flows preempt long flows, and receive full link bandwidth. Short flows therefore achieve near-optimal completion time. We verified it in the FCT logs but omit the details because of page limitations. After the short flows complete, more bandwidth becomes available to the long flows, allowing them to finish quickly. The minDist placement outperforms minLoad placement because it minimizes the total network load, defined as sum of the product of the size and the hop count for each flow. In contrast, when the network follows the Fair policy (Figure 2.4(b)), short flows no longer preempt long flows. The minLoad placement works better – especially for long flows – because it ensures that long flows avoid being placed on nodes with existing long flows. However, Figure 2.4(b) shows that short flows may suffer longer FCTs under the minLoad placement compared to the minDist placement. This usually happens when newly arriving long flows are placed on nodes with ongoing short flows, thus increasing the FCTs of short flows. In conclusion, this experiment demonstrates that the performance of task placement depends on the underlying network scheduling policy. Therefore, it is important to design a task placement framework that takes into account the underlying network scheduling policy.

2.3   Bandwidth Allocation in Multi-tenant Datacenters

2.3.1   *Related Work*

We can divide the related work based on the objective.

Latency Sensitive (LS): Silo [Jang *et al.* (2015)] proposes a placement algorithm and a hypervisor-based packet pacing to provide latency guarantees. However, it does not differentiate among flows and applications with other performance goals such as deadlines and relative priorities among flows. HULL [Alizadeh *et al.* (2012)] trades bandwidth for ultra-low latency and it requires modification to switch ASIC. Fastpass [Perry *et al.* (2014)] uses a centralized arbiter to decide when and which path each packet should be sent. Its potential in large scale datacenters is yet to be proven. QJUMP [Grosvenor *et al.* (2015)] uses multiple physical switch queues to provide different combinations of latency and throughput. It supports both latency-sensitive and throughput-sensitive flows, but with constraints. DCTCP can keep switch queue length at a low level to reduce packet latency [Alizadeh *et al.* (2011)].

Deadline Sensitive (DS): D^3 pioneers the idea of incorporating deadline awareness into network scheduling [Wilson *et al.* (2011b)]. However, D^3 and RACS [Munir *et al.* (2013a)] are not deployment friendly as they require modifications to the commodity switch hardware. D^2TCP [Vamanan *et al.* (2012b)] is a distributed deadline-sensitive protocol, which uses both ECN feedback and deadlines to modulate the congestion window.

Completion Sensitive (CS): PDQ [Hong *et al.* (2012b)] uses preemptive flow scheduling to minimize average FCT. pFabric [Alizadeh *et al.* (2013b)] and PASE [Munir *et al.* (2014)] assume flow size is known a priori, and attempt to approximate Shortest Job First (SJF), which is the optimal scheduling for minimizing average FCT in a single bottleneck scenario. L²DCT [Munir *et al.* (2013c)] and PIAS [Bai *et al.* (2015)], without prior knowledge of flow size information, reduce AFCT by approximating the Least Attained Service (LAS) scheduling discipline.

2.3.2 *Motivation: Interference when Sharing Network*

To demonstrate interference, when flows with different objectives coexist in the same network, we use a single bottleneck topology as shown in Fig. 2.5(a). This represents a common datacenter scenario where edge to core links might be the bottleneck among flows of different applications. We set the switch ECN marking threshold to 20, the switch buffer size to 250 packets and the round trip time to 300 us. We consider traffic from a LS application (from $SRC1$ to $DST1$), a DS application (from $SRC2$ to $DST2$), and a CS application (from $SRC3$ to $DST3$). We use the instantaneous end-to-end packet RTT, fraction of missed deadlines, and average FCT (AFCT) as the performance metrics for evaluating the LS, DS and CS flows, respectively. We use NS-2 for performance evaluation.

We consider state-of-the-art deployment-friendly protocols for each of the performance goals and implement them in NS-2. Specifically, we use DCTCP for LS flows, D²TCP for DS and L²DCT for CS flows. For LS flows, we generate small (2 KB) flows that arrive at intervals following a Poisson distribution and require an aggregate bandwidth of 400 Mbps on average. For DS and CS, the flows are generated uniformly within the range 2 KB-198 KB with deadlines in the range 5-25 ms (for DS only). Flows arrive at intervals generated following Poisson distribution and incurring low (20%), medium(50%) and high (80%) load on the link.

2.3.2.1 *Performance in Isolation*

We first evaluate the application performance in a scenario where each protocol has exclusive access to the underlying network. When used in isolation, we represent flows as Base-LS, Base-DS, and Base-CS respectively. In these experiments, the bottleneck link capacity is 500 Mbps.

Base-LS: As shown in Fig. 2.5(b), the LS flow packets experience almost zero queuing delay and the round-trip latency is very close to the RTT (300 us).

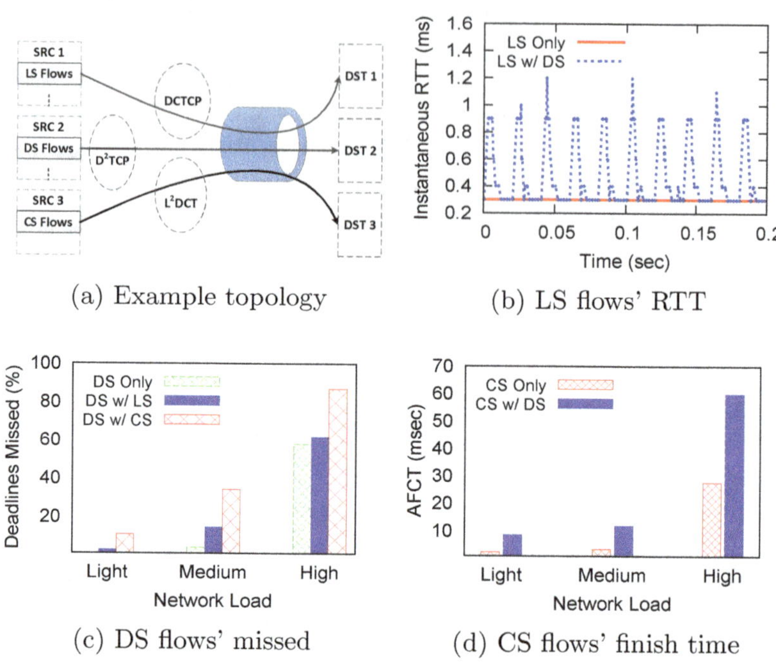

(a) Example topology   (b) LS flows' RTT

(c) DS flows' missed   (d) CS flows' finish time

Fig. 2.5   Interference demonstration, when alone and coexist.

Base-DS: Fig. 2.5(c) demonstrates the deadline missing rate of DS flows across a range of loads. We can see that for light to moderate loads, almost no flows miss deadlines. However, at high load many flows miss deadlines. *Base-CS:* Fig. 2.5(d) shows the AFCT under different network load conditions.

2.3.2.2   *Coexistence of Different Objectives*

Next, we evaluate the scenarios with two performance objectives coexisting in the network. The bottleneck link capacity is 1000 Mbps, which is large enough to meet the demands of both types of flows.

Coexist-LS/DS: In this scenario, the performance of LS flows is severely affected as shown in Fig. 2.5(b). LS flows experience large queuing delays and, as a result, their tail latency increases by more than 300%; the average latency increases by more than 50%. On the other hand, DS flows also experience performance degradation and many flows miss their deadlines, as shown in Fig. 2.5(c).

Coexist-DS/CS: We consider the coexistence of DS and CS flows in the network. In this scenario, DS flows experience performance degradation, as shown in Fig. 2.5(c): even at low loads, some of the flows miss their deadline due to interference from CS flows and the degradation increases up to 4x for medium and higher network loads. Similarly, the completion times of CS flows is also affected and flows take longer to finish compared to the scenario with only CS flows in the network (Fig. 2.5 (d)). Specifically, at higher loads, the AFCT of CS flows increases by more than 2x.

2.3.2.3 *Same Objective Different Tenants*

We also consider the scenarios where multiple tenants with the same performance objective coexist. We evaluate both *Coexist-LS/LS* and *Coexist-DS/DS* scenarios, where the bottleneck capacity is not large enough to meet the requirements of all flows. Lacking the ability to favor one tenant over another, flows of both the tenants experience performance degradation. We omit results due to space limitation.

2.3.3 *Motivation: Current Isolation won't Work*

An intuitive solution is to segregate application flows with different objectives to separate physical queues in a switch. Such an segregation approach requires a large number of traffic classes, which are not supported by currently available CoS tags in packet formats; existing commodity switches also do not have sufficient number of queues [Shieh *et al.* (2011)].

Bandwidth Guarantee: Several bandwidth guarantee approaches have been proposed, which provide network abstraction models and placement algorithms for tenants or applications to express their bandwidth requirements [Guo *et al.* (2010); Shieh *et al.* (2011); Rodrigues *et al.* (2011); Jeyakumar *et al.* (2013a); Popa *et al.* (2013); Lee *et al.* (2014)]. Bandwidth guarantee are coarse grained: they should meet the peak requirements, which is either inefficient, or is suboptimal in terms of flow objectives.

Proportional Sharing: Seawall provides per-entity weight enforcement for each VM-to-VM tunnel [Shieh *et al.* (2011)]. However, it does not support bandwidth allocation at flow-level granularity, hence cannot optimize the performance objectives of individual flow divisions. Further, it does not support tenant level network sharing.

Chapter 3

A Near-Optimal Transport for Datacenters

In this chapter, we present the design and analysis of a near-optimal datacenter transport called PASE. PASE is a transport framework that synthesizes the three transport strategies, namely in-network **P**rioritization, **A**rbitration, and **S**elf-adjusting **E**ndpoints. The underlying design principle behind PASE is that each transport strategy should focus on what it is best at doing, such as:

- Arbitrators should do inter-flow prioritization at coarse time-scales. They should not be responsible for computing precise rates or for doing fine-grained prioritization.
- Endpoints should probe for any spare link capacity on their own, without involving any other entity. Further, given their lack of global information, they should not try to do inter-flow prioritization (protocols that do this have poor performance, as shown in Section 2).
- In-network prioritization mechanism should focus on per-packet prioritization at short, sub-RTT timescales. The goal should be to obey decisions made by other strategies while keeping the data plane simple and efficient.

Switch	Vendor	Num. Queues	ECN
BCM56820 [bro (2014)]	Broadcom	10	Yes
G8264 [ibm (2014)]	IBM	8	Yes
7050S [ari (2014)]	Arista	7	Yes
EX3300 [jun (2014)]	Juniper	5	No
S4810 [del (2014)]	Dell	3	Yes

Given the above roles for each strategy, the high-level working of PASE is as follows. Every RTT, each source invokes the arbitration algorithm to get its *priority queue* and *reference rate*. The arbitration decision is based on the flows currently in the system and their priorities (e.g., deadline, flow-size). As the name suggests, the reference rate is not binding on the sources, so depending on the path conditions, the sources may end up sending at higher or lower than this rate (i.e., self-adjusting endpoints). A key benefit of PASE is that we do not require any changes to the data plane: switches on the path use existing priority queues to schedule packets and employ explicit congestion notification (ECN) to signal congestion. As shown in Table 3.1, most modern switches support these two features.

To achieve high performance while being deployment friendly, PASE incorporates two key components: a control plane arbitration mechanism and an end-host transport protocol. While existing arbitration mechanisms operate in the data plane (and hence require changes to the network fabric), we implement a separate control plane for performing arbitration in a scalable manner. To this end, we introduce optimizations that leverage the typical tree structure of datacenter topologies to reduce arbitration overhead. Finally, PASE's transport protocol has an explicit notion of reference rate and priority queues, which leads to new rate control and loss recovery mechanisms.

In the following sections, we describe the control plane and the end-host transport protocol of PASE, followed by the details of its implementation.

3.1   Arbitration Control Plane

While a centralized arbitrator is an attractive option for multiple reasons, making it work in scenarios involving short flows is still an open problem [Al-Fares *et al.* (2010); Curtis *et al.* (2011)]. Prior work [Hong *et al.* (2012a)] shows that the problem of flow arbitration can indeed be solved in a distributed fashion: each switch along the path of a flow independently makes the arbitration decision and returns the allocated rate for its own link, and the source can pick the minimum rate. While prior work implements arbitration as part of the data plane, PASE supports this as part of the control plane because experiences with prior protocols (e.g., XCP [Katabi *et al.* (2002)]) show that even small changes to the data plane are hard to deploy.

We now describe (a) the basic arbitration algorithm employed by *each* PASE arbitrator in the control plane and the key sources of overhead that limit the scalability of the arbitration process, (b) how arbitrators exchange information to determine the priority queue and the reference rate for each flow across the end-to-end path, and (c) two optimizations that reduce the arbitration overhead by exploiting the characteristics of typical datacenter topologies.

3.1.1 *Basic Arbitration Algorithm*

For each link in the datacenter topology, there is an arbitrator that runs the arbitration algorithm and makes decisions for all flows that traverse the particular link. The arbitrator can be implemented on any server in the datacenter or on dedicated controllers that are co-located with the switches. The arbitration algorithm works at the granularity of a flow, where a flow could be a single RPC in a typical client-server interaction, or a long running TCP-like connection between two machines.

Algorithm 1 Arbitration Algorithm

Input: $< FlowSize, FlowID, demand(optional) >$
Output: $< PrioQue, R_{ref} >$
Arbitrator locally maintains a sorted list of flows
Step#1: Sort/update flow entry based on the $FlowSize$
Step#2: Compute $PrioQue$ and R_{ref} of the flow.
//Link capacity is C, and AggregateDemandHigher (ADH) is the sum of demands of flows with priority higher than current flow.
1: Assign rate:
if $ADH < C$ **then**
    $R_{ref} = min(demand, C - ADH)$;
else
    $R_{ref} = baserate$;
end if
2: Assign $PrioQue$:
$PrioQue = \lceil ADH/C \rceil$;
if $PrioQue > LowestQueue$ **then**
    $PrioQue = LowestQueue$;
end if
3: return $< PrioQue, R_{ref} >$;

The interaction between a flow's source and the arbitrator(s) is captured in Algorithm 1. The source provides the arbitrator(s) with two pieces of information: i) the flow size ($FlowSize$), which is used as the criterion for scheduling (i.e., shortest flow first). To support other scheduling techniques, the $FlowSize$ can be replaced by deadline [Wilson *et al.* (2011a)] or task-id for task-aware scheduling [Dogar *et al.* (2014b)] and ii) demand, this represents the maximum rate at which the source can send data. For long flows that can saturate the link, this is equal to the NIC rate, while for short flows that do not have enough data to saturate the link, this is set to a lower value. Demand and flow size are inputs to the arbitration algorithm whereas the flows' reference rate (R_{ref}) and priority queue ($PrioQue$) is the output.

To compute R_{ref} and $PrioQue$, the arbitrator locally maintains a sorted list of flows based on their sizes. This list is updated based on the latest *FlowSize* information of the current flow. The flow's priority queue and reference rate depend on the aggregate demand (AggregateDemandHigher or ADH) of flows that have higher priority compared to the current flow. An ADH value less than the link capacity C implies that there is some spare capacity on the link and the flow can be mapped to the top queue. Thus, if the flow's demand is less than the spare capacity, we set the reference rate equal to the demand. Otherwise, we set the reference rate equal to the spare capacity.

The other case is when the ADH exceeds link capacity. This happens when a link is already saturated by higher priority flows, so the current flow cannot make it to the top queue. In this case, the flow's reference rate is set to a base value, which is equal to one packet per RTT. This allows such low priority flows to make progress in case some capacity becomes available in the network, and to even increase their rate in the future based on self-adjusting behavior.

Finally, if the current flow cannot be mapped to the top queue, it is either mapped to the lowest queue (if ADH exceeds the aggregate capacity of intermediate queues) or is mapped to one of the intermediate queues. Thus, each intermediate queue accommodates flows with an aggregate demand of C and the last queue accommodates all the remaining flows.

Challenges. The above design described how each arbitrator determines the priority queue and reference for a flow at a particular *link*. To carry out arbitration across the *end-to-end path* of a flow, we design a distributed control plane for arbitration. There are three sources of overhead that limit the scalability of such a distributed control plane.

- *Communication Latency.* The communication latency between the source and the arbitrator depends on their physical distance within the datacenter. This delay matters the most during flow setup time as it can end up increasing the FCT, especially for short flows. To keep this delay small, arbitrators must be placed carefully, such

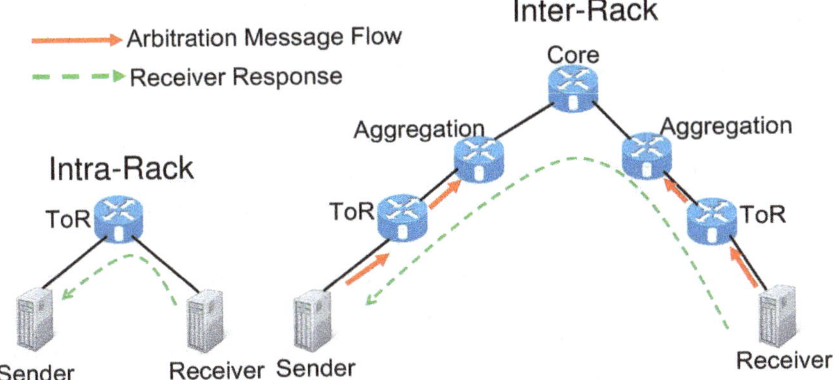

Fig. 3.1 The *bottom-up* arbitration approach employed by PASE for intra-rack and inter-rack traffic scenarios.

that they are located as close to the sources as possible.

- *Processing Overhead.* The second challenge is the processing overhead of arbitration messages, which can potentially add non-negligible delay, especially under high load scenarios.
- *Network Overhead.* Due to a separate control plane, each arbitration message is potentially processed as a separate packet by the switches which consumes link capacity. We need to ensure that this overhead is kept low and that it does not cause network congestion for our primary traffic.

To reduce these overheads, PASE's distributed control plane has been structured to carry out arbitration in a bottom-up manner, which we describe next.

3.1.2 *Bottom Up Arbitration*

We exploit the typical tree structure of datacenter topologies. Sources obtain information about the *PrioQue* and R_{ref} in a bottom-up fashion, starting from the leaf nodes up to the core as shown in Figure 3.1. For this purpose, the end-to-end path between a source and destination is divided into two halves—one from the source up to the root (`srcHalf`) and the other from the destination up to the root (`dstHalf`).

For each half, the respective leaf nodes (i.e., source and destination) initiate the arbitration at the start of a flow[1]. They start off with their link to the ToR switch and then move upwards. The arbitration request messages move up the arbitration hierarchy until it reaches the top-level arbitrator. The responses move downwards in the opposite direction. A source receives arbitration responses for the `srcHalf` and the `dstHalf` containing priority queue and reference rate assigned to the flow. A source then uses the minimum of these reference rates and the lowest of the priority queues assigned by arbitration at the `srcHalf` and the `dstHalf`.

This bottom-up approach ensures that for intra-rack communication, arbitration is done solely at the endpoints. Thus, in this scenario, flows incur no additional network latency for arbitration. This is particularly useful as many datacenter applications have communication patterns that have an explicit notion of rack affinity [Alizadeh *et al.* (2010); Benson *et al.* (2010)].

For the inter-rack scenario, the bottom up approach facilitates two other optimizations, *early pruning* and *delegation*, to reduce the arbitration overhead and latency. Both early pruning and delegation exploit a trade-off between low overhead and high accuracy of arbitration. As our evaluation shows, by giving away some accuracy, they can significantly decrease the arbitration overhead.

Early Pruning   The network and processing overheads can be reduced by limiting the number of flows that contact the arbitrators for *PrioQue* and R_{ref} information. In early pruning, only flows that are mapped to the highest priority queue move upwards for arbitration. Thus, in Algorithm 1 a lower-level arbitrator only sends the arbitration message to its parent if the flow is mapped to the top queue(s). This results in lower priority flows being pruned at lower levels, as soon as they are mapped to lower priority queues (see Figure 3.2(a)). The intuition behind this is that a flow mapped to a lower priority queue on one of its links will never make it to the highest priority queue irrespective of the arbitration decision on other links. This is because a flow always uses the lowest of the priority queues assigned by all the arbitrators (i.e., bottleneck in the path). Thus, we avoid the overhead of making arbitration decisions for the flows mapped to lower priority queues.

There are two key benefits of early pruning. First, it reduces the network overhead as arbitration messages for only high priority flows propagate

---

[1]The destination node initiates the arbitration when it receives an arbitration request message from the source node.

upwards. Second, it reduces the processing load on higher level arbitrators. In both cases, the reduction in overhead can be significant, especially in the more challenging heavy load scenarios, where such overhead can hurt system performance.

In general, early pruning makes the overhead independent of the total number of flows in the system. Instead, the overhead depends on the number of children that a higher level arbitrator may have because each child arbitrator only sends a limited number of flows (the top ones) upwards. Due to limited port density of modern switches (typically less than 100), the number of children, and hence the overhead, is quite small. This leads to significant reduction in the overhead compared to the non-pruning case where the overhead is proportional to the total number of flows traversing a link, which can be in thousands (or more) for typical datacenter settings [Alizadeh *et al.* (2010); Benson *et al.* (2010)]. However, the above overhead reduction comes at the cost of less precise arbitration. As we only send the top flows to the higher-level arbitrators, flows that are pruned do not get the complete and accurate arbitration information. Our evaluation shows that sending flows belonging to the top two queues upwards (rather than just the top queue), provides the right balance: there is little performance degradation while reduction in overhead is still significant.

Delegation Delegation is specially designed to reduce the arbitration latency. While early pruning can significantly reduce the arbitration processing overhead as well as the network overhead, it does not reduce the latency involved in the arbitration decision because top flows still need to go all the way up to the top arbitrator.

In delegation, a higher level link (i.e., closer to the core) is divided into smaller "virtual" links of lower capacity – each virtual link is delegated to one of the child arbitrators who then becomes responsible for all arbitration decisions related to the virtual link. Thus, it can make a local decision about a higher level link without going to the corresponding arbitrator. On each virtual link, we run the same arbitration algorithm i.e., Algorithm 1 as we do for normal links.

As a simple example, the aggregation-core link of capacity C shown in Figure 3.2(b) can be divided into N virtual links of capacity a_iC each (where a_i is the fraction of capacity allocated to virtual link i) and then delegated to one of the child arbitrators. The capacity of each virtual link is updated periodically, reflecting the *PrioQue* of flows received by each child arbitrator. For example, one child that is consistently observing flows

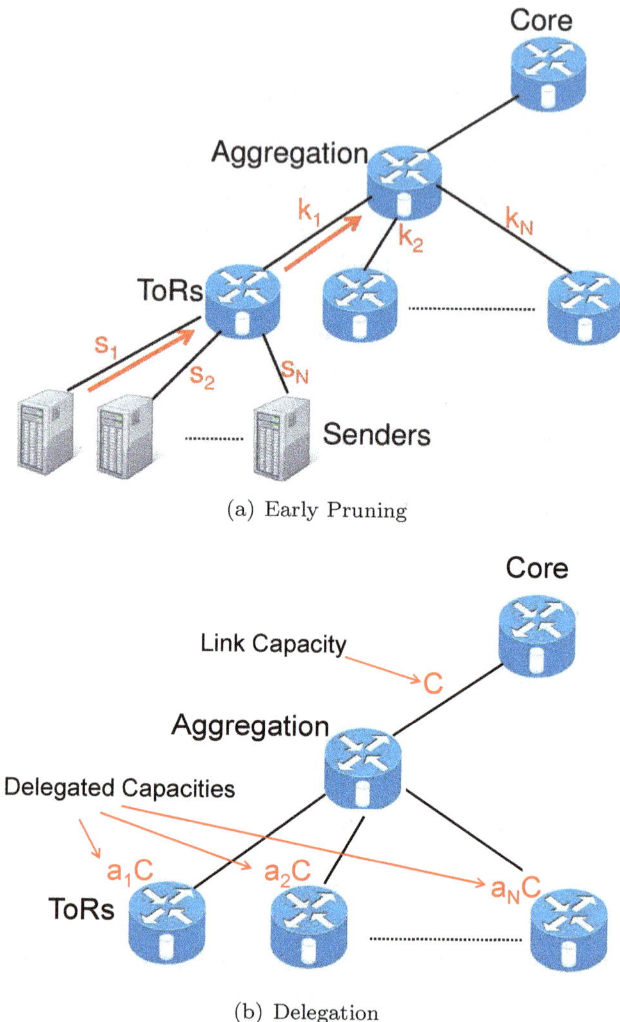

(a) Early Pruning

(b) Delegation

Fig. 3.2 (a) The *early pruning* optimization used to reduce the arbitration overhead. Note that s_i and k_i represent flows that are mapped to the highest priority queue at the senders and the ToR arbitrators, respectively and (b) the *delegation* optimization used to reduce the setup latency and control overhead.

of higher priorities can get a virtual link of higher capacity.

Delegation provides two benefits. First, it reduces the flow setup delay because arbitration decisions for higher level links are made at lower level arbitrators, which are likely to be located close to the sources (e.g., within the rack). Second, it reduces the control traffic destined towards higher level arbitrators. Note that this happens because only *aggregate* information about flows is sent by the child arbitrators to their parents for determining the new share of virtual link capacities.

The impact on processing load has both positive and negative dimensions. While it reduces the processing load on higher level arbitrators, it ends up increasing the load on lower level arbitrators as they need to do arbitration for their parents' virtual links too. However, we believe this may be acceptable as lower level arbitrators typically deal with fewer flows compared to top level arbitrators.

Like early pruning, delegation also involves the overhead-accuracy trade-off. The capacity assigned to a specific virtual link may not be accurate which may lead to performance degradation. For example, we may have assigned a lower virtual capacity to a child who may suddenly start receiving higher priority flows. These flows would need to wait for an update to the virtual link capacity before they can get their due share. On the other hand, there could be cases where the virtual capacity may remain unused if the child does not have enough flows to use this capacity. This is especially true in scenarios where a link is delegated all the way to the end-host and the end-host may have a bursty flow arrival pattern.

Given the above trade-off, PASE only delegates the Aggregation-Core link capacity to its children (ToR-Aggregation arbitrators). These child arbitrators should be typically located within the rack of the source/destination (or co-located with the ToR switch). Thus, for any inter-rack communication within a typical three level tree topology, the source and destination only need to contact their ToR-aggregation arbitrator, who can do the arbitration all the way up to the root. In fact, flows need not wait for the feedback from the other half i.e., destination-root. Thus, in PASE, a flow starts as soon as it receives arbitration information from the child arbitrator. This approach is reasonable in scenarios where both halves of the tree are likely to have similar traffic patterns. If that is not true then PASE's self-adjusting behavior ensures that flows adjust accordingly.

3.2　End-host Transport

PASE's end-host transport builds on top of existing transports that use the self-adjusting endpoints strategy (e.g., DCTCP). Compared to existing protocols, the PASE transport has to deal with two new additional pieces: (a) a priority queue (*PrioQue*) on which a flow is mapped and (b) a reference sending rate (R_{ref}). This impacts two aspects of the transport protocol: rate control and loss recovery. Rate control in PASE is more guided and is closely tied to the R_{ref} and the *PrioQue* of a flow. Similarly, the transport requires a new loss recovery mechanism because flows mapped to lower priority queues may experience spurious timeouts as they have to wait for a long time before they get an opportunity to send a packet. We now elaborate on these two aspects.

Rate Control: A PASE source uses the R_{ref} and the *PrioQue* assigned by the arbitrators to guide its transmission rate. The rate control uses congestion window (*cwnd*) adjustment, based on the R_{ref} and the flow RTT, to achieve the average reference rate at RTT timescales.

Algorithm 2 describes the rate control mechanism in PASE. For the flows mapped to the top queue, the congestion window is set to $R_{ref} \times RTT$ in order to reflect the reference rate assigned by the arbitrator. For all other flows, the congestion window is set to one packet. Note that for flows belonging to the top queue, the reference rate R_{ref} is generally equal to the access link capacity unless flows have smaller sizes.

For the flows mapped to lower priority queues (except the bottom queue), the subsequent increase or decrease in congestion window *cwnd* is

---

Algorithm 2 Rate Control

Input: $< PrioQue, R_{ref} >$
Output: $< cwnd >$ // congestion window
// Priority queues q_1, q_2,.., q_k where q_1 is the highest priority queue and q_2, q_3, and q_{k-1} are intermediate queues
// if an ACK with the ECN-Echo flag set is received
if $ACK_{marked} == 1$ **then**
   $cwnd = cwnd \times (1 - \alpha/2)$; // Use DCTCP decrease law
else
  if $PrioQue == q_1$ **then**
    $cwnd = R_{ref} \times RTT$;
    $isInterQueue = 0$; // not an intermediate queue
  else if $PrioQue \in \{q_2, q_3, .., q_{k-1}\}$ **then**
    // if already mapped to an intermediate queue
    if $isInterQueue == 1$ **then**
      $cwnd = 1 + 1/cwnd$; // Use DCTCP increase law
    else
      $isInterQueue = 1$; $cwnd = 1$;
    end if
  else if $PrioQue == q_k$ **then**
    $cwnd = 1$; $isInterQueue = 0$;
  end if
end if

---

based on the well-studied control laws of DCTCP [Alizadeh *et al.* (2010)]. In particular, when an unmarked ACK is received, the window size is increased as

$$cwnd = cwnd + 1/cwnd. \tag{3.1}$$

When a marked ACK (i.e., with ECN-Echo flag set) is received, the window size is reduced as

$$cwnd = cwnd \times (1 - \alpha/2) \tag{3.2}$$

where α is the weighted average of the fraction of marked packets. This self-adjusting behavior for higher priority queues is important for ensuring high fabric utilization at all times because the R_{ref} may not be accurate and there may be spare capacity or congestion along the path.

For the flows mapped to the bottom queue, the window size always remains one. This is because under high loads all flows that cannot make it to the top queues are mapped to the bottom queue, so the load on the bottom queue can be usually high.

Loss Recovery: For flows belonging to the top queue, we use existing loss recovery mechanisms (i.e., timeout based retransmissions). However, flows that get mapped to the lower priority queues can timeout for two reasons: (a) their packet(s) could not be transmitted because higher priority queues kept the link fully utilized and (b) a packet was lost. In case of scenario (a), a sender should avoid sending any new packets into the network as it increases the buffer occupancy and the likelihood of packet losses especially at high network loads. In case of scenario (b), a sender should retransmit the lost packet as early as it is possible so that the flows can make use of any available capacity without under-utilizing the network. However, differentiating between these two scenarios is a challenging task without incurring any additional overhead.

We use small probe packets instead of retransmitting the entire packet whenever a flow, mapped to one of the lower priority queues, times out. If we receive an ACK for the probe packet (but not the original packet), it is a sign that the data packet was lost, so we retransmit the original data packet. If the probe packet is also delayed (no ACK received), we increase our timeout value (and resend another probe) just like we do this for successive losses for data packets. An alternative approach is to set suitable timeout values: smaller values for flows belonging to the top queue and larger values for the other flows.

Finally, a related issue is that of *packet reordering*. When a flow from a low priority queue gets mapped to a higher priority queue, packet reordering may occur as earlier packets may be buffered at the former queue.

This can lead to unnecessary backoffs which degrades throughput. To address this, we ensure that when a flow moves to a higher priority queue, we wait for the ACKs of already sent packets to be received before sending packets with the updated priority.

3.3   Discussion

Handling arbitrator failures: When an arbitrator fails, the arbitration result can be inaccurate, which may lead to network congestion (e.g., if the reference rate is greater than the available capacity). To handle such scenarios, PASE sources fall back to applying DCTCP control laws upon detecting the failure of one or more arbitrators along a flow's path. In addition, such flows are mapped to the top queue to avoid starvation of flows. When the arbitrator becomes alive again, the source arbitrator detects this within the arbitration period (equal to one RTT), and the end-to-end arbitration resumes. As each arbitration message carries flow state information, arbitrators can rebuild the sorted list of flows as soon as arbitration messages are received.

Handling losses of arbitration messages: Loss of arbitration messages can negatively impact the arbitration process. Thus, we use TCP SACK for reliably sending arbitration messages. Moreover, to ensure that arbitration messages get delivered in a timely manner, they are mapped to the highest priority queue.

Overhead of arbitration messages: The size of each arbitration message is 52 bytes (including 40 bytes of TCP and IP headers). Sending 52-byte messages every RTT$=300\mu$s equates to a sending rate of $\approx$1.4Mbps. On a 1Gbps and 10Gbps links, this amounts to only 0.14% and 0.014% of overhead, respectively. With the delegation optimization, arbitration messages do not percolate beyond the ToR-Aggregation arbitrators, which prevents such control traffic from aggregating at higher level links. With early pruning, arbitration decision is only carried out for flows that are mapped to the top queues. This further limits the control traffic[2].

---

[2]In our evaluation, the path BDP was 38KB. Even if a single source generates 38 1KB flows every RTT, this would lead to a control traffic overhead of 0.53% on a 10Gbps link.

3.4 Performance Evaluation and Comparison

3.4.1 *Implementation*

We implement PASE on a small-scale Linux testbed as well as in the ns2 simulator. Our ns2 implementation supports all the optimizations discussed in Section III whereas our testbed implementation only supports the basic arbitration algorithm that runs on the endhosts (src/dest only) and we do not implement separate (external) arbitrators for our Linux implementation.

Client: For the testbed evaluation, we implement the transport protocol and the arbitration logic as Linux kernel modules on the clients. The Linux transport module, which is built on top of DCTCP, communicates with the arbitration module to obtain the packet priority and the reference rate. It then adds the PASE header on outgoing packets. For ns2 evaluation, we implement client side similar to the Linux implementation, however, additionally the arbitration module at the client communicates with the arbitrator that is co-located with the ToR switch. The arbitration module communicates with the arbitrator using packets containing PASE header.

Arbitrator: The arbitration module implements Algorithm 1. It maintains a sorted list of flows based on flowSize or flowDeadline and assigns a priority queue and reference rate using the logic described in Algorithm 1. It returns these values to the arbitration module running on clients, which communicate with rate control module to control flow' priority.

Switch: For the desired switch support, we use the PRIO [qpr (2006)] queue and CBQ (class-based queueing) implementation, on top of the RED queue implementation in Linux and ns2. We use eight priority queues/classes and classify packets based on the DSCP field in the IP header. Out of these eight queues, a separate, strictly lower priority queue is maintained for background traffic. For the RED queue, we set the low and high thresholds of RED queue to K and perform marking based on the instantaneous rather than the average queue length as done in DCTCP [Alizadeh *et al.* (2010)].

3.5 Evaluation

We evaluate the performance of PASE using ns2 simulations [ns2 (2006)] as well as through small-scale testbed experiments. First, we conduct macrobenchmark experiments in ns2 to compare PASE's performance against existing datacenter transports. We compare PASE against both deployment-friendly protocols including DCTCP [Alizadeh *et al.* (2010)], D^{2}TCP [Vamanan *et al.* (2012a)], and L^{2}DCT [Munir *et al.* (2013b)] (§3.6.1) as well as the best performing transport, namely, pFabric [Alizadeh *et al.* (2013a)] (§3.6.2). Second, we micro-benchmark the internal working of PASE (e.g., benefits of arbitration optimizations, use of reference rate, etc) using simulations (§3.7).

Data center Topology: We use a 3-tier topology for our evaluation comprising layers of ToR (Top-of-Rack) switches, aggregation switches, and a core switch. This is a commonly used topology in datacenters [Al-Fares *et al.* (2008); Vamanan *et al.* (2012a); Wilson *et al.* (2011a)]. The topology interconnects 160 hosts through 4 ToR switches that are connected to 2 aggregation switches, which in turn are interconnected via a core switch. Each host-ToR link has a capacity of 1 Gbps whereas all other links are of 10 Gbps. This results in an oversubscription ratio of 4:1 for the uplink from the ToR switches. In all the experiments, the arbitrators are co-located with their respective switches. The end-to-end round-trip propagation delay (in the absence of queueing) between hosts via the core switch is $300\mu s$.

Traffic Workloads: We consider traffic workloads that are derived from patterns observed in production datacenters. Flows arrive according to a Poisson process and flow sizes are drawn from the interval [2 KB, 198 KB] using a uniform distribution, as done in prior studies [Hong *et al.* (2012a); Wilson *et al.* (2011a)]. This represents query traffic and latency sensitive short messages in datacenter networks. In addition to these flows, we generate two long-lived flows in the background, which represents the 75th percentile of multiplexing in datacenters [Alizadeh *et al.* (2010)]. Note that we always use these settings unless specified otherwise. We consider two kinds of flows: *deadline-constrained flows* and *deadline-unconstrained flows*. They cover typical application requirements in today's data centers [Vamanan *et al.* (2012a)].

We also evaluate PASE under the web search [Alizadeh *et al.* (2010)] and data mining [Alizadeh *et al.* (2013a)] workloads. Compared to web search, the data mining is much more skewed, with ∼80% of flows having a size of less than 10KB and the largest 3.5% of flows containing more than 95% of all bytes.

Protocols Compared: We compare PASE with several data center transports including DCTCP [Alizadeh *et al.* (2010)], D^{2}TCP [Vamanan *et al.* (2012a)], L^{2}DCT [Munir *et al.* (2013b)], and pFabric [Alizadeh *et al.*

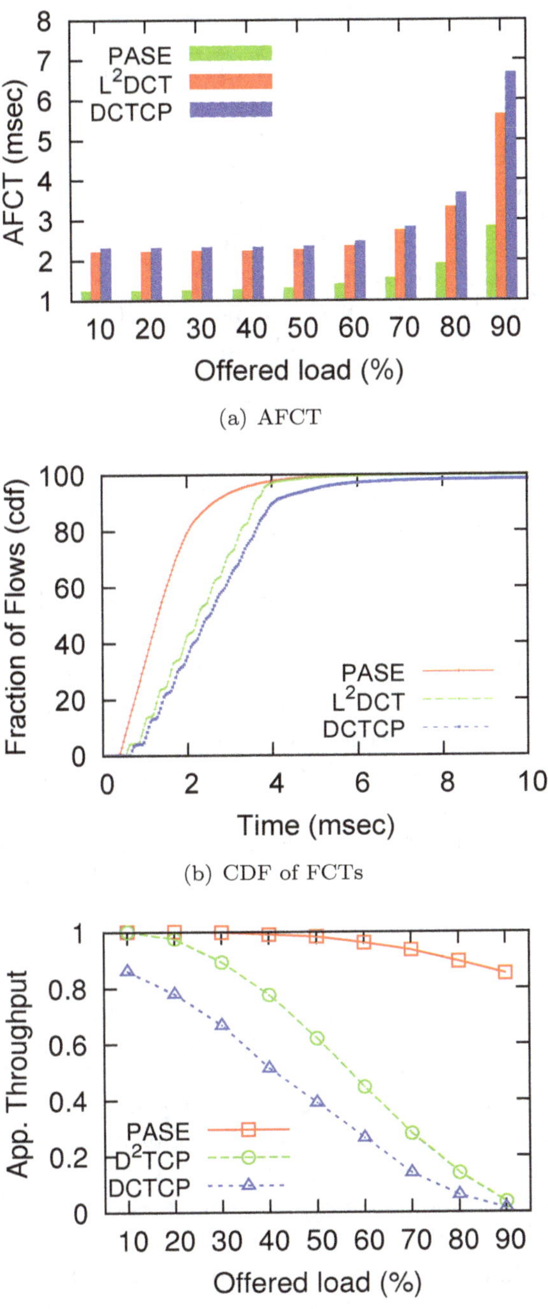

(a) AFCT

(b) CDF of FCTs

(c) Application Throughput

Fig. 3.3 (a) Comparison of PASE with L^{2}DCT and DCTCP in terms of AFCTs under the (*left-right*) inter-rack scenario, (b) shows the CDF of FCTs at 70% load in case of (a), and (c) Deadline-constrained flows: Comparison of application throughput for PASE, D^{2}TCP and DCTCP under the intra-rack scenario.

Scheme	Parameters
DCTCP	qSize = 100 pkts (packet size is 1KB)
D^{2}TCP	markingThresh = 65 pkts (10Gbps) & 20 pkts (1Gbps)
L^{2}DCT	minRTO = 10ms, initCwnd = 10 pkts
pFabric	qSize = 76 pkts (= 2×BDP)
	initCwnd = 38 pkts (= BDP)
	minRTO = 1ms (∼3.3×RTT)
PASE	qSize = 100 pkts
	minRTO (flows in top queue) = 10ms
	minRTO (flows in other queues) = 200ms
	numQue = 8

(2013a)]. We implemented DCTCP, D^{2}TCP and L^{2}DCT in ns2 and use the source code of pFabric provided by the authors to evaluate their scheme. The parameters of these protocols are set according to the recommendations provided by the authors, or reflect the best settings, which we determined experimentally (see Table 4.1).

Performance Metrics: For traffic without any deadlines, we use the FCT as a metric. We consider the AFCT as well as the 99th percentile FCT for small flows. In case of web search and data mining workloads, we report the AFCT across all flows as well as separately for short and long flows. For deadline-constrained traffic, we use application throughput as our metric which is defined as the fraction of flows that meet their deadlines. We use the control messages per second to quantify the arbitration overhead.

3.6   Macro-benchmarks

3.6.1   *Comparison with Deployment Friendly Schemes*

PASE is a deployment friendly transport that does not require any changes to the network fabric. Therefore, we now compare PASE's performance with deployment friendly data center transports, namely, DCTCP and L^{2}DCT. DCTCP [Alizadeh *et al.* (2010)] is a *fair sharing* protocol that uses ECN marks to infer the degree of congestion and employs adaptive backoff factors to maintain small queues. The goal of L^{2}DCT [Munir *et al.* (2013b)] is to minimize FCT – it builds on DCTCP by *prioritizing* short flows over long flows through the use of adaptive control laws that depend on the size of the flows.

Deadline-unconstrained flows: We consider an inter-rack communication scenario (termed as *left-right*) where 80 hosts in the left subtree of the core switch generate traffic towards hosts in the right subtree. This is a common scenario in user-facing web services where the front-end servers and the back-end storage reside in separate racks [Zats *et al.* (2012b)]. The generated traffic comprises flows with sizes drawn from the interval [2 KB, 198 KB] using a uniform distribution. In addition, we generate two long-lived flows in the background.

Figure 3.3(a) shows the improvement in AFCT as a function of network load. Observe that PASE outperforms L^{2}DCT and DCTCP by at least 50% and 70%, respectively across a wide range of loads. At low loads, PASE performs better primarily because of its quick convergence to the correct rate for each flow. At higher loads, PASE ensures that shorter flows are *strictly* prioritized over long flows, whereas with L^{2}DCT, all flows, irrespective of their priorities, continue to send at least one packet into the network. This lack of support for strict priority scheduling in L^{2}DCT leads to larger FCTs for short flows. DCTCP does not prioritize short flows over long flows. Thus, it results in worst FCTs across all protocols.

Figure 3.3(b) shows the CDF of FCTs at 70% load. Observe that PASE results in better FCTs for almost all flows compared to L^{2}DCT and DCTCP.

Deadline-constrained flows: We now consider latency-sensitive flows that have specific deadlines associated with them. Thus, we compare PASE's performance with D^{2}TCP, a deadline-aware transport protocol. We replicate the D^{2}TCP experiment from [Vamanan *et al.* (2012a)], which considers an intra-rack scenario with 20 machines and generate short query traffic with flow sizes drawn from the interval [100 KB, 500 KB] using a uniform distribution. Figure 3.3(c) shows the application throughput as a function of network load. PASE significantly outperforms D^{2}TCP and DCTCP, especially at high loads because of the large number of active flows in the network. Since each D^{2}TCP and DCTCP flow sends at least one packet per RTT, these flows consume significant network capacity which makes it difficult for a large fraction of flows to meet their respective deadlines. PASE, on the other hand, ensures that flows with the earliest deadlines are given the desired rates and are strictly prioritized inside the switches.

3.6.2 *Comparison with Best Performing Scheme*

We now compare the performance of PASE with pFabric, which achieves close to optimal performance in several scenarios but requires changes in switches. With pFabric, packets carry a priority number that is set independently by each flow. Based on this, pFabric switches perform priority-based scheduling and dropping. All flows start at the line rate and backoff only under persistent packet loss. PASE performs better than pFabric in two important scenarios: (a) multi-link (single rack) scenarios with all-to-all traffic patterns and (b) at high loads (generally $> 80\%$) whereas it achieves similar performance ($< 6\%$ difference in AFCTs) compared to pFabric in the following two cases: (a) single bottleneck scenarios and (b) when the network load is typically less than 80%.

We first consider the *left-right* inter-rack scenario where the aggregation-core link becomes the bottleneck. Figure 3.4 shows the AFCT and 99th percentile FCT as a function of load. Observe that PASE achieves AFCT similar to pFabric (Figure 3.4(a)) and for 99th percentile FCT (Figure 3.4(b)) pFabric achieves smaller FCT for up to 50% load and PASE achieves comparable performance. However, at $\geq 60\%$ loads, PASE results in smaller FCT than pFabric. At 90% load, this improvement is more than 85%. This happens due to high and persistent loss rate with pFabric at high loads.

Next we consider an all-to-all intra-rack scenario, which is common in applications like web search where responses from several worker nodes within a rack are combined by an aggregator node before a final response is sent to the user. Moreover, any node within a rack can be an aggregator node for a user query and the aggregators are picked in a round robin fashion to achieve load balancing [Abts and Felderman (2012)].

Figure 3.5 shows that PASE provides up to 85% improvement in 99th percentile FCT over pFabric (Figure 3.5(b)) and results in lower AFCTs across *all* loads (Figure 3.5(a)). This happens because with pFabric multiple flows sending at line rate can collide at a downstream ToR-host link. This causes a significant amount of network capacity to be wasted on the host-ToR links, which could have been used by other flows (as this is an all-to-all scenario). With PASE, flows do not incur any arbitration latency in the intra-rack scenario as new flows start sending traffic at line rate based on the information (priority and reference rate) from their local arbitrator. After one RTT, all flows obtain their global priorities which helps in avoiding any persistent loss of throughput in case the local and global priorities are different.

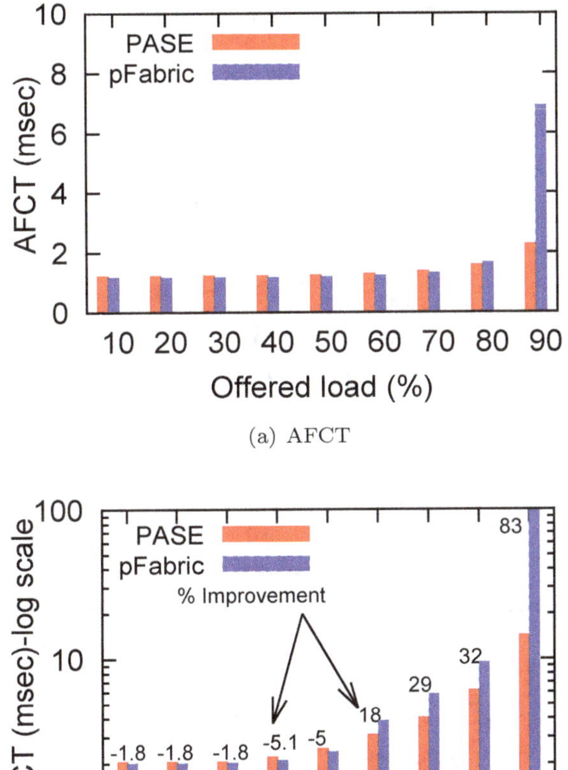

(a) AFCT

(b) 99th percentile

Fig. 3.4 Comparison of PASE and pFabric for inter-rack scenario: a) AFCT, b) 99th percentile with % gain of PASE over pFabric.

3.6.3 *Evaluation under the Web Search and Data Mining Workloads*

We now evaluate PASE's performance under the web search [Alizadeh *et al.* (2010)] and data mining [Alizadeh *et al.* (2013a)] workloads and perform comparison with DCTCP, L^2DCT and pFabric. These empirical workloads contain a diverse mix of short and long flows with heavy-tailed characteristics. In the web search workload, more than 95% of all bytes are from the

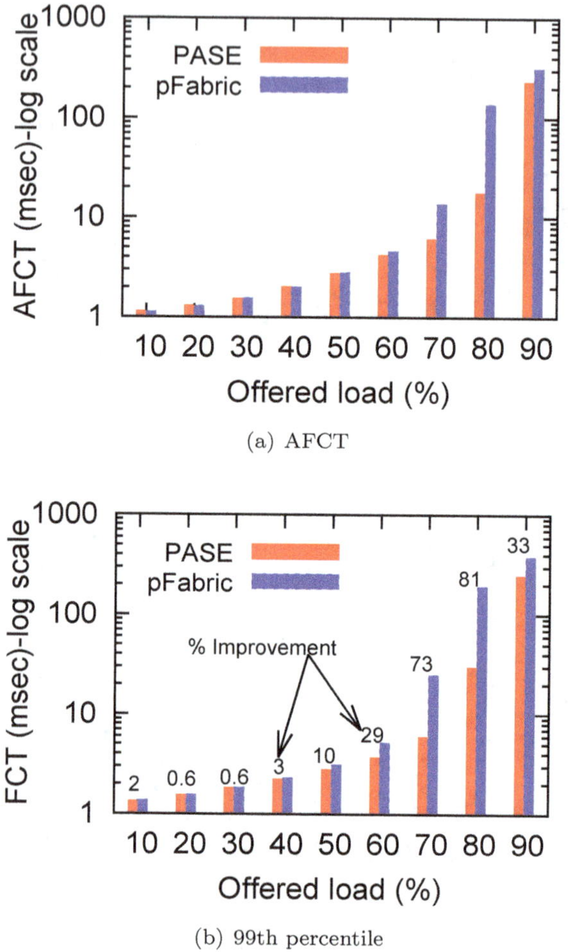

(a) AFCT

(b) 99th percentile

Fig. 3.5   Comparison of PASE and pFabric intra-rack scenario: a) AFCT, b) 99th percentile with % gain of PASE over pFabric.

30% of the flows with sizes in the range [1,20]MB. The data mining workload is more skewed: ~80% of the flows are less than 7KB in size and 95% of all bytes are in the 4% flows that are larger than 35MB. Note that the data mining workload leads to large number of tiny flows. PASE's arbitration may incur greater overhead in this case (as large number of flows get mapped to the top queue) as well as inflate the AFCT of short flows (due to the arbitration latency being a greater fraction of their FCTs). Thus, it is important to evaluate how PASE performs under such workloads.

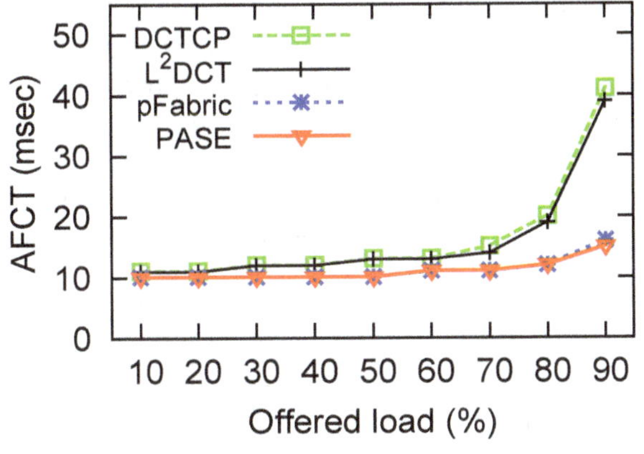

(a) Web search workload

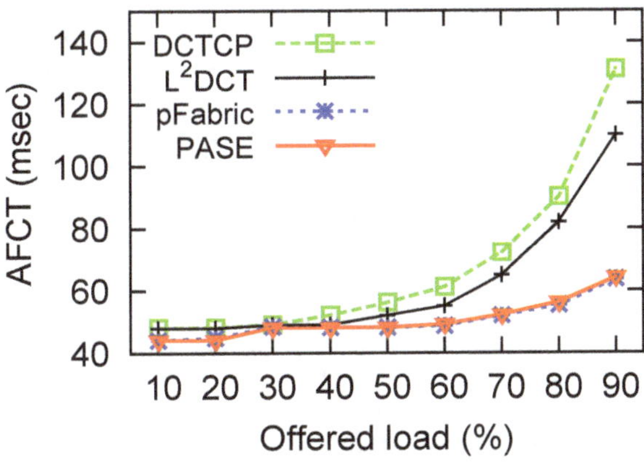

(b) Data mining workload

Fig. 3.6 Comparison of PASE with pFabric, L^{2}DCT and DCTCP under web search and data mining workloads.

We consider the *left-right* inter-rack scenario, where the aggregation-core link becomes the bottleneck. Figure 3.6 shows the AFCT as a function of load under the data mining and web search workloads. Observe that PASE consistently outperforms DCTCP and L^{2}DCT and achieves similar performance compared to pFabric across *all* loads. Note that using a larger initial window size (=10) in case of DCTCP and L^{2}DCT improves performance but lack of in-networking priority scheduling and arbitration leads to large AFCTs especially under medium to high loads. Figure 3.7 and 3.9

shows the breakdown of AFCT across small and large flows the same scenario. Observe that PASE not only achieves similar performance to pFabric for flows less than 100KB (i.e., short flows), it improves the AFCT of long flows under the web search workload. This happens because long flows with PASE experience lower packet loss rate than pFabric. These results show that PASE achieves comparable or better performance than the existing state-of-the-art protocols, like pFabric, yet does not require any changes to the switch hardware.

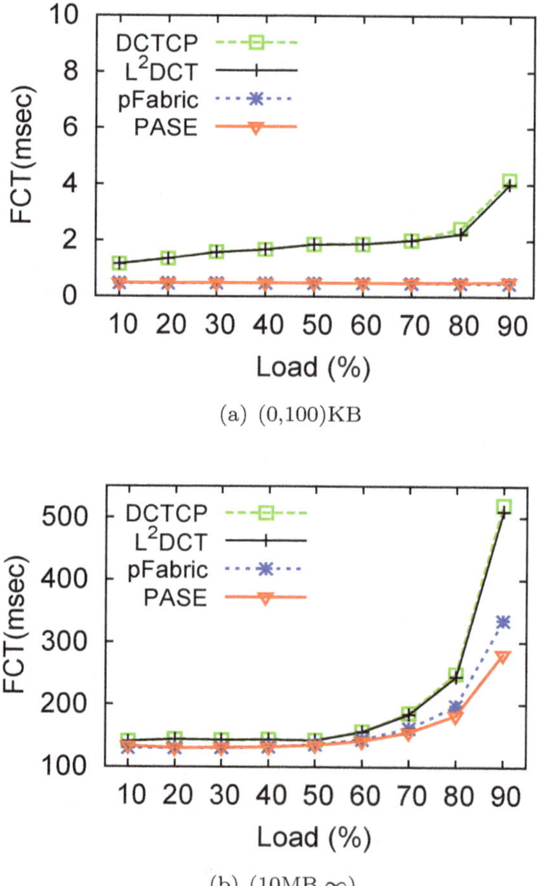

(a) (0,100)KB

(b) (10MB,∞)

Fig. 3.7   AFCT comparison of PASE with pFabric, L^2DCT and DCTCP under the web search workload. Note: the y-axis of plots have different ranges.

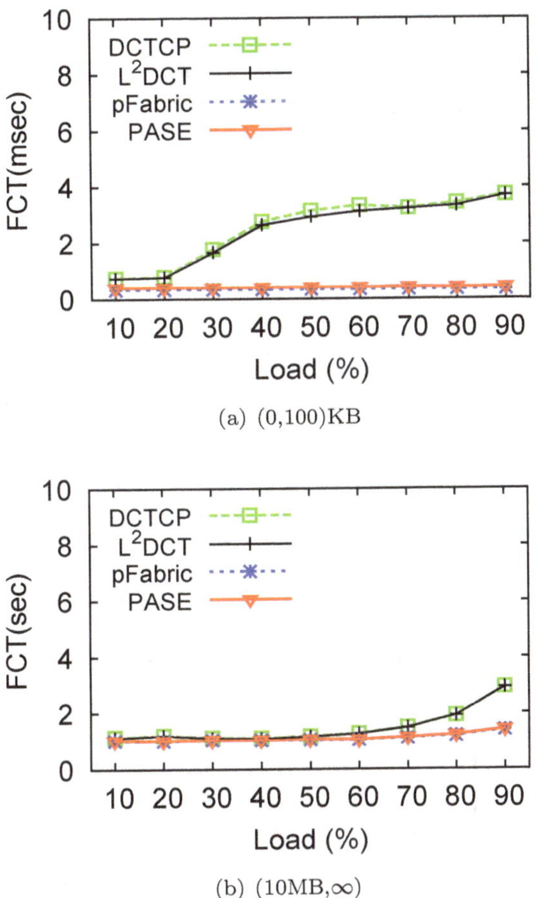

(a) (0,100)KB

(b) (10MB,∞)

Fig. 3.8   AFCT comparison of PASE with pFabric, L^{2}DCT and DCTCP under the data mining workload. Note that y-axis of plots have different labels.

3.6.4   *PASE under the Incast scenario*

We now evaluate PASE under synchronized flow arrivals, which are fairly common in datacenters due to the *partition-aggregate* structure followed by many datacenter applications [Alizadeh *et al.* (2010); Nishtala *et al.* (2013)]. We generate multiple synchronized short flows with sizes uniformly distributed between 50KB and 150KB and vary the number of flows from 2 to 100 (where each flow originates from exactly one sender). Figure 3.9(a) shows that PASE performs well across a range of conditions.   PASE is able to tolerate large packet bursts as it maps only those flows to the high priority queues that can saturate the link and maps rest of the flows to the lower priority queues. As a result PASE essentially eliminates network congestion and substantially improves AFCT.

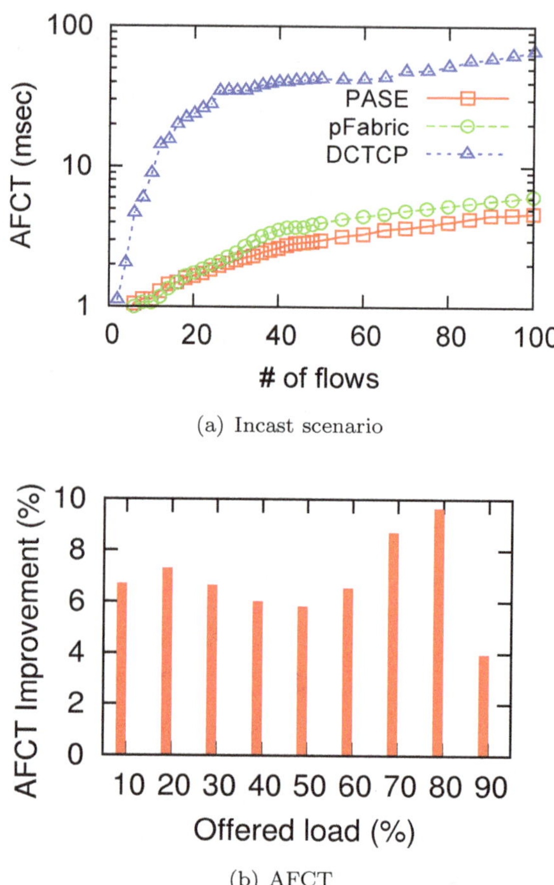

(a) Incast scenario

(b) AFCT

Fig. 3.9   Performance of PASE under (a) incast scenario and (b) AFCT improvement due to PASE optimizations as a function of offered load.

3.7   Micro-benchmarks

In this section, we evaluate the basic components of PASE with the help of several micro-benchmarks. Results show that PASE optimizations significantly reduce the control traffic overhead and the number of messages that arbitrators need to process. In addition, other features of PASE such as its rate control are important for achieving high performance.

3.7.1 *Arbitration Optimizations*

PASE introduces early pruning and delegation for reducing the arbitration overhead of update messages. We now evaluate the overhead reduction brought about by these optimizations as well as study their impact on the performance of PASE. Figure 3.10(a) shows the overhead reduction that is achieved by PASE when all its optimizations are enabled. Observe that these optimizations provide up to 50% reduction in arbitration overhead especially at high loads. This happens because when these optimizations are enabled, higher-level arbitrators delegate some portion of the bandwidth to lower level arbitrators, which significantly reduces the control overhead on ToR-Aggregation links. In addition, updates of only those flows are propagated that map to the highest priority queues due to early pruning. Figure 3.9(b) shows that these optimizations also improve the AFCT by 4-10% across all loads. This happens because of delegation, which reduces the arbitration delays.

Benefit of end-to-end arbitration: PASE enables global prioritization among flows through its scalable end-to-end arbitration mechanism. This arbitration, however, requires additional update messages to be sent on the network. It is worth asking if most of the benefits of PASE are realizable through only local arbitration, which can be solely done by the endpoints. Thus, we now compare the performance of end-to-end arbitration and local arbitration in the *left-right* inter-rack scenario. Figure 3.10(b) shows that end-to-end arbitration leads to significant improvements (up to 60%) in AFCTs across a wide range of loads. This happens because local arbitration cannot account for scenarios where contention does not occur on the access links, thus leading to sub-optimal performance.

In PASE, sources contact the arbitrators periodically, every RTT. The `Arbitration=OFF` case can also be viewed as (a) a scenario in which the arbitration period is so large that none of the short flows get any end-to-end arbitration feedback during their lifetime or (b) a scenario in which one or more arbitrators have failed. As a result, a source cannot get any end-to-end arbitration feedback. Instead, only the local arbitrator (i.e., the one at the end-host) assigns a priority and rate to a flow based on the host-ToR link. Figure 3.10(b) shows that even in such cases, PASE outperforms DCTCP.

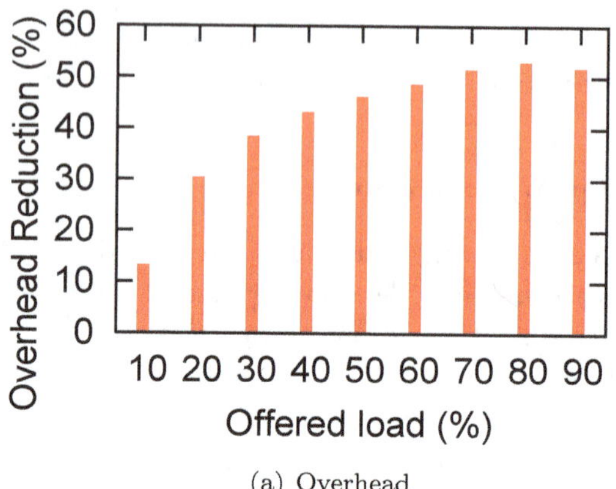

(a) Overhead

(b) AFCT

Fig. 3.10   AFCT improvement and overhead reduction as a function of load for PASE with its optimizations in the *left-right* scenario.

3.7.2   *In-network Prioritization and Transport Micro-benchmarks*

In this section, we evaluate the impact of different components in PASE.

Impact of switch buffer size: We now evaluate the impact of reducing the switch buffer size. Figure 3.11(a) shows the AFCT for two switch buffer sizes (i.e., 100 packets and 500 packets). Observe that for loads less than 70%, the AFCT remains unchanged. However, at higher loads the AFCT increases by up to 9% at 90% load. These results show that even with small buffer sizes, PASE keeps AFCTs small.

Impact of number of priority queues: We now evaluate the impact

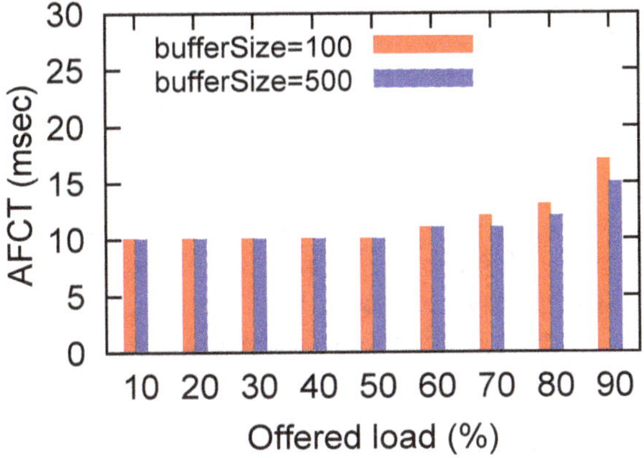

(a) Impact of switch buffer size

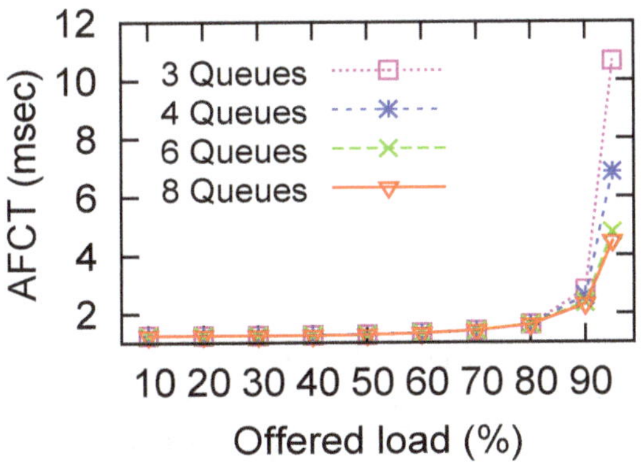

(b) Priority Queues

Fig. 3.11   (a) PASE with varying switch buffer size and (b) PASE with varying number of priority queues (*left-right* scenario).

of changing the number of priority queues in the switches. To test this scenario we repeat the *left-right* inter-rack scenario with different number of queues. Figure 3.11(b) shows that using four queues provide significant improvement in AFCT at loads $\geq 70\%$. However, increasing the number of queues beyond this provides only marginal improvement in AFCT. These results further reinforce the ability of PASE to achieve high performance with existing switches that support a limited number of priority queues.

Reference Rate: We now evaluate the benefit of using the reference rate information. We compare PASE with PASE-DCTCP, where *all* flows (including the ones mapped to the top queue as well as the lowest priority queue) behave as DCTCP sources and do not use the reference rate. However, these flows are mapped to different priority queues through the normal arbitration process. To illustrate this, we consider the intra-rack scenario with 20 nodes and uniformly distributed flow sizes from [100 KB, 500 KB]. As shown in Figure 3.13(a), leveraging reference rate results in AFCTs of PASE to be 50% smaller than the AFCTs for PASE-DCTCP.

Impact of RTO and Probing: Flows mapped to the lower priority queues may experience large number of timeouts, which can affect performance. We implement probing in which flows mapped to the lowest priority queue send a header-only probe packet every RTT rather than a full-sized packet. Using probing improves performance by $\approx 2.4\%$ and $\approx 11\%$ at 80% and 90% loads, respectively in the all-to-all intra-rack scenario. Note that unlike pFabric, PASE does not require small RTOs which forgoes the need to have high resolution timers.

3.8   Distributed vs. Centralized Arbitration

In this section, we compare the performance of PASE under a single centralized arbitrator (which makes decisions for all flows in the DC network) with (multiple) distributed arbitrators. For distributed arbitration, we use the same settings as mentioned in Section 4.6. Our evaluation shows that distributed arbitration improves AFCT under both the *all-to-all* and *left-to-right* traffic scenarios (see Figure 3.12). Under distributed arbitration, local arbitrators (that are close to the sources) can assign priorities to the sources and flows start sending data without waiting for feedback from other arbitrators along the path. This reduces the arbitration latency and improves AFCT. In the centralized approach, the arbitrator may not be located close to *all* sources, which can significantly increase the arbitration latency for some traffic. To study the impact of controller/arbitrator placement under the centralized approach, we consider placing the arbitrator at aggregation and core levels (i.e., co-located with the switches). The evaluation results in Figure 3.12) show that the application performance improves by up to 50% when a centralized arbitrator is placed at the aggregation switch level as compared to when placed at core switch level.

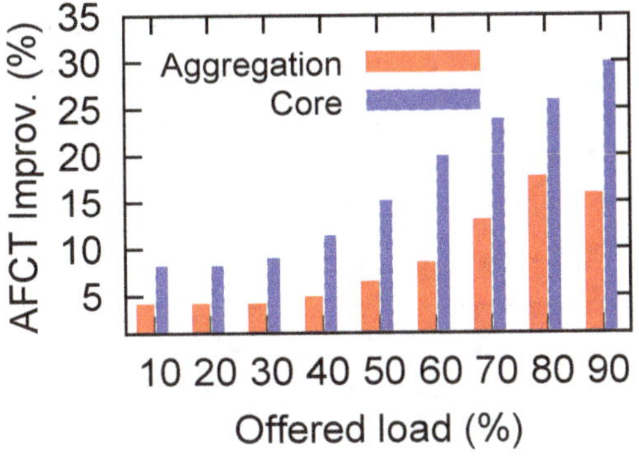

(a) Intra-rack scenario

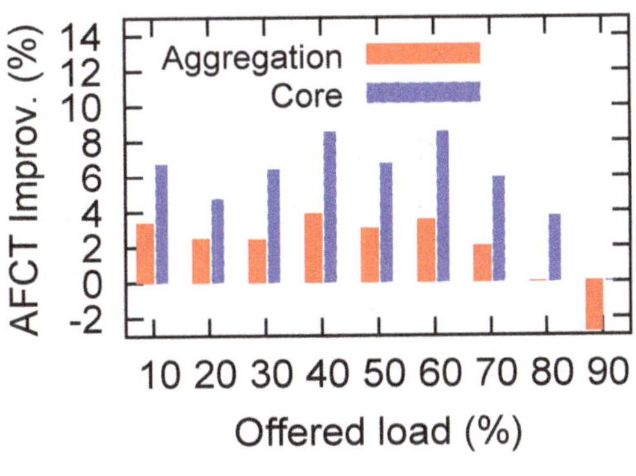

(b) Inter-rack scenario

Fig. 3.12   AFCT improvement under distributed arbitration over centralized arbitration under (a) intra-rack scenario (b) inter-rack scenario.

3.9   Testbed Evaluation

We now present a subset of results from our testbed evaluation. Our testbed comprises of a single rack of ten nodes (nine clients, one server), with 1 Gbps links, $250\,\mu$sec RTT and a queue size of 100 packets on each interface. We set the marking threshold K to 20 packets and use eight priority queues. We compare PASE's performance with the DCTCP implementation (provided by its authors). To emulate data center like settings, we generate flows sizes that are uniformly distributed between 100 KB and 500 KB, as done in [Vamanan *et al.* (2012a)]. We start 1000 short flows and vary the flow arrival rate to generate a load between 10% to 90%. In addition, we also generate a long lived background flow from one of the clients. We compare PASE with DCTCP and report the average of ten runs. Figure 3.13(b) shows the AFCT for both the schemes. Observe that PASE significantly outperforms DCTCP: it achieves ≈50%-60% smaller AFCTs compared to DCTCP. This also matches the ns2 simulation results.

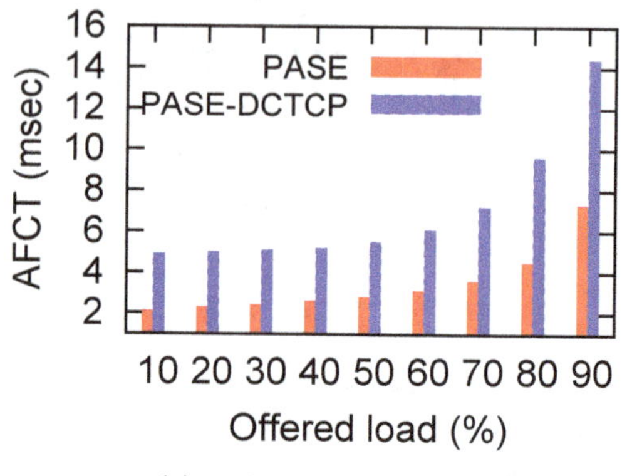

(a) PASE vs PASE-DCTCP

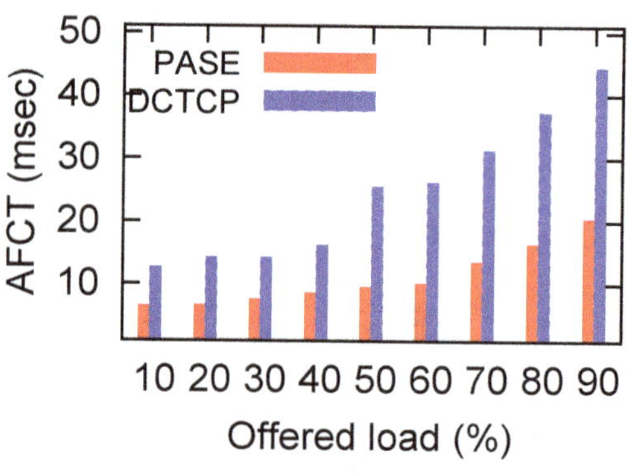

(b) Testbed Evaluation

Fig. 3.13   PASE AFCT performance.

3.10 Conclusion

In this chapter, we discussed three key ideas. First, we extract the three underlying strategies used in data center transport protocols and find that these strategies, which were used individually in earlier transports, are in fact complementary to each other and can be unified to work together.

Second, we design PASE, a data center transport protocol that synthesizes existing transport strategies. PASE includes two new components: a scalable arbitration control plane for data center networks, and an endpoint transport protocol that is explicitly aware of priority queues and uses a guided rate control mechanism. Third, we conducted a comprehensive evaluation of PASE, which includes both macro-benchmarks that compare PASE's performance against multiple existing transport protocols, and micro-benchmarks that focus on the internal working of the system.

Chapter 4

Task Placement in Datacenters

In this chapter, we present the design and analysis of NEAT, which is a **N**etwork-sch**E**duling-**A**ware **T**ask placement framework that considers the *network scheduling policy* and the *network state* while making task placement decisions. NEAT considers placing both flows and coflows in the network via placing the tasks on the nodes that act as destinations of these flows (coflows). The placement framework, coupled with the underlying network scheduling policy (e.g., Fair, FCFS, LAS, SRPT), ensures that network resources are properly allocated among tasks to minimize their average completion time.

NEAT uses a distributed architecture to make task placement decisions, as shown in Figure 4.1. It leverages the master-slave architecture of existing task scheduling systems [Hindman *et al.* (2011); Vavilapalli *et al.* (2013)] to achieve its functionality in a distributed fashion. NEAT has two components, i) a global task placement daemon and ii) a per-node network daemon. The two components exchange information to perform network-aware task scheduling.

Network Daemon: NEAT network daemon (similar to node manager in Hadoop) runs on all the nodes (i.e., endhosts) in the network and uses the completion time of data transfer (FCT for flow, CCT for coflow) as a metric for predicting task performance. The prediction is based on the network state, e.g., (residual) sizes of all active flows, and the network scheduling policy. Therefore, network daemon performs two functions: (i) maintaining network information of all the active tasks on the node (such as the number of flows and their residual sizes), and ii) predicting the performance of a new task when requested by the task placement daemon, based on the analysis in section 4.1. NEAT considers only the edge links for task performance prediction. Therefore, the task performance prediction

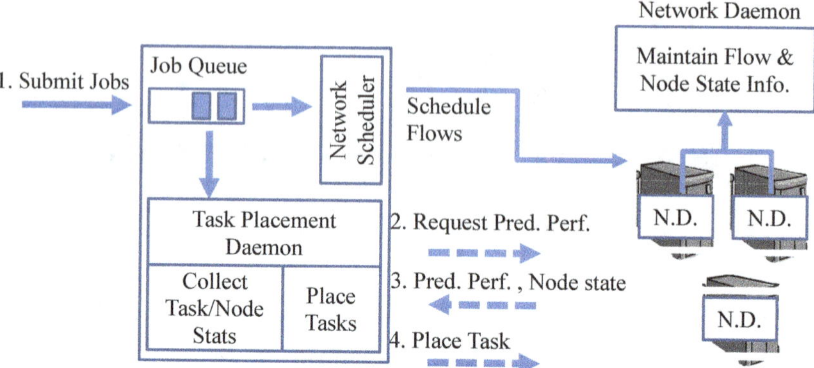

Fig. 4.1   NEAT components.

is based on the assumption that only the edge links are bottleneck in the network and core is congestion free. As a result NEAT needs to maintain flow information at the end-hosts only and does not require any feedback from the network.

Task Placement Daemon: NEAT task placement daemon makes placement decisions in two steps: First, it queries the network daemons on nodes that are valid hosts (determined by node state, CPU and memory) of a given task for their predicted task performance. Next, it chooses the best node or subset of nodes for placing the task using the predicted task completion times and node states (i.e., the smallest residual flow size of active tasks on each node). It also caches the node states locally to facilitate future placement decisions, as discussed below. The node states cache is updated whenever a new task is placed on the node or an existing task is completed.

NEAT Workflow: As illustrated in Figure 4.1, when the task placement daemon receives a request to place a new task (step 1), it identifies a set of preferred hosts based on local copies of node states and contacts the respective network daemons to get predicted performance of the new task (step 2). Each network daemon maintains the local network state (such as the number and the sizes of flows starting/ending at the node) and uses this state together with knowledge of the network scheduling policy to predict the performance of the new task. The task placement daemon then gathers this information (step 3) and places the task on the best of the preferred hosts based on the predicted performance (step 4).

Discussions: It is worthwhile to clarify a few points. First of all, NEAT is a task placement framework and as such, it does not impose any changes in the network switches or network scheduling mechanism. The network congestion is managed by the underlying network scheduling policy. However, NEAT helps to mitigate the network congestion by properly distributing traffic loads across the network. Moreover, in the current design, NEAT abstracts network as a single-switch topology, as assumed in earlier works [Jalaparti *et al.* (2015); Alizadeh *et al.* (2013b)]. The single-switch assumption means that only edge links are the bottleneck and thus for task completion time (FCT/CCT) prediction, it only considers edge links. However, such restriction is not fundamental to NEAT, and we discuss in Section 4.10 how it can be extended to other topologies.

In the next two sections, we discuss task performance prediction and NEAT design in more detail.

4.1 Task Performance Predictor

NEAT has a pluggable task performance predictor that can predict the completion time of a given task under an arbitrary network scheduling policy. An interesting insight of our analysis is that: for flow-based scheduling, it suffices to predict FCT according to the Fair policy under mild conditions even if the underlying policy is not Fair; for coflow-based scheduling, however, this is generally not true.

From a networking perspective, placing a task onto a server is equivalent to placing a flow onto a path (or a coflow onto a set of paths). We now define the objective function for flow placement; the objective function for coflow placement is analogous. For flow placement, our goal is to place each flow onto the path that minimizes the sum (and hence average) FCT over all active flows. Consider a flow f placed on path p_f with size s_f (bits). Let $\mathrm{FCT}(f, l)$ denote the completion time of flow f on link $l \in p_f$ (i.e., time taken for the flow to finish transmission over link l). Now consider placing a new flow f_0 onto path p_{f_0}. Let $\Delta\mathrm{FCT}(f, l)$ denote the increase in the completion time of f on link l due to the scheduling of f_0. Let F be the set of cross-flows in the network (i.e., flows that share at least one link with f_0). Then the increase in the sum FCT over all active flows due to the placement of f_0 equals

$$\max_{l \in p_{f_0}} \mathrm{FCT}(f_0, l) + \sum_{f \in F} \left(\max_{l \in p_f} (\mathrm{FCT}(f, l) + \Delta\mathrm{FCT}(f, l)) \right.$$

$$\left. - \max_{l \in p_f} \mathrm{FCT}(f, l) \right), \qquad (4.1)$$

and the optimal online placement is to place f_0 such that (4.1) is minimized (note that (4.1) depends on p_{f_0}).

The original objective (4.1) requires calculation of the FCT before and after placing f_0 for every flow $f \in F$ and every hop l traversed by f. To simplify computation, we exchange the order of summation and maximization to obtain an alternative objective function

$$\max_{l \in p_{f_0}} \mathrm{FCT}(f_0, l) + \max_{l \in p_{f_0}} \sum_{f \in F_l} \Delta\mathrm{FCT}(f, l)$$

$$\geq \max_{l \in p_{f_0}} \left(\mathrm{FCT}(f_0, l) + \sum_{f \in F_l} \Delta\mathrm{FCT}(f, l) \right), \qquad (4.2)$$

where F_l is the set of flows traversing link l. Note that (4.2) is only an approximation of (4.1) and thus minimizing (4.2) is not guaranteed to minimize the sum FCT. However, as we show later, the alternative objective (4.2) has a nice property that it is invariant, up to a constant scaling, to the network scheduling policy under certain conditions (see Propositions 4.1 and 4.2), and the placement that minimizes (4.2) achieves superior performance in minimizing the FCT for a variety of flows and network scheduling policies.

For simplicity of analysis, we do not consider the impact of future task arrivals or task completion on the prediction. We choose this design in favor of applicability (not requiring prediction capability) and stability (not moving existing flows) of NEAT design (see remark § 4.4.1).

4.2   FCT Prediction for Flow Scheduling

Given a placement of flow f_0 and its cross-flows, the FCT of f_0 is determined by the scheduling policy employed by the network. We therefore study FCT prediction under several widely-adopted scheduling policies, including FCFS, Fair, LAS, and SFF. For ease of presentation, we fix a (candidate) placement and consider the prediction for a given link l with bandwidth B_l. The key idea of NEAT predictor is to compute the total number of bytes that will be transmitted across the bottleneck link by the time the current flow finishes transmission, which is then divided by the link bandwidth to predict the completion time of the current flow. For example, to predict the completion time of a flow f when placed onto a path p, we compute for each link l on p the total traffic volume V_l from f and coexisting flows that will cross l upon the completion of f, and then the maximum of V_l/B_l (B_l is the bandwidth of l) over all the links $l \in p$ gives the predicted completion time of f. This approach applies to any work-conserving scheduling policy (i.e., a link is never idle when there is pending traffic on that link), while different policies differ in the computation of V_l.

4.2.1 *FCT under FCFS Scheduling*

Under FCFS scheduling, flows are served in the order they arrive, and FCT of the new flow can be predicted as:

$$\mathrm{FCT}^{\mathrm{FCFS}}(f_0, l) = \frac{1}{B_l}(s_{f_0} + \sum_{f \in F_l} s_f), \tag{4.3}$$

and $\Delta\mathrm{FCT}^{\mathrm{FCFS}}(f, l) \equiv 0$ for all $f \in F_l$ since the new flow does not affect the completion of existing flows. Hence, the two objectives in (4.1) and (4.2) coincide in this case, both equal to $\max_{l \in p_{f_0}} \mathrm{FCT}^{\mathrm{FCFS}}(f_0, l)$.

4.2.2 *FCT under Fair or LAS Scheduling*

Under a scheduling policy that performs fair sharing, all flows will receive equal service until completion, i.e., by the time flow f_0 completes transmission over link l, each existing flow $f \in F_l$ will have transmitted $\min(s_f, s_{f_0})$ bytes over l. The FCT of f_0 can thus be predicted as:

$$\mathrm{FCT}^{\mathrm{FAIR}}(f_0, l) = \frac{1}{B_l}\left(s_{f_0} + \sum_{f \in F_l} \min(s_f, s_{f_0})\right). \tag{4.4}$$

Meanwhile, the fair sharing rule implies that for each flow $f \in F_l$ of size $s_f < s_{f_0}$, scheduling f_0 increases its FCT by imposing an additional traffic load of s_f on link l (during the lifetime of f); for each flow $f \in F_l$ of size $s_f \geq s_{f_0}$, f_0 will finish earlier, causing an additional load of s_{f_0}. Thus, the change in FCT of existing flows is:

$$\Delta\mathrm{FCT}^{\mathrm{FAIR}}(f, l) = \frac{\min(s_f, s_{f_0})}{B_l}. \tag{4.5}$$

Substituting (4.4) and (4.5) into (4.1) gives the overall increase in the sum FCT.

The alternative objective (4.2) accepts a more compact form in this case. Specifically, for given l,

$$\text{FCT}^{\text{FAIR}}(f_0, l) + \sum_{f \in F_l} \Delta\text{FCT}^{\text{FAIR}}(f, l)$$

$$= \frac{s_{f_0}}{B_l} + \frac{2}{B_l} \sum_{f \in F_l} \min(s_f, s_{f_0}) \approx 2\text{FCT}^{\text{FAIR}}(f_0, l), \tag{4.6}$$

where the approximation is accurate when s_{f_0} is small relative to $\sum_{f \in F_l} \min(s_f, s_{f_0})$.

Remark: Since LAS scheduling (with preemption) is equivalent to fair sharing, the above result also applies to LAS scheduling.

4.2.3 *FCT under SRPT Scheduling*

If the network employs SRPT scheduling, then only flows of remaining sizes smaller than or equal to the current flow will be served before the current flow finishes (assuming FCFS rule is applied to break ties among flow sizes), and larger flows will be preempted. Hence, the FCT of the new flow f_0 under SRPT can be predicted as:

$$\text{FCT}^{\text{SRPT}}(f_0, l) = \frac{1}{B_l} \left(s_{f_0} + \sum_{f \in F_l : s_f \leq s_{f_0}} s_f \right). \tag{4.7}$$

Meanwhile, each flow of size $s_f > s_{f_0}$ will be delayed by s_{f_0}/B_l due to the placement of f_0, while flows of size $s_f \leq s_{f_0}$ will not be affected, implying:

$$\Delta\text{FCT}^{\text{SRPT}}(f, l) = \frac{s_{f_0}}{B_l} \mathbb{1}_{s_f > s_{f_0}}, \tag{4.8}$$

where $\mathbb{1}.$ is the indicator function. Applying (4.7) and (4.8) to (4.1) gives the first objective. For second objective, we have

$$\text{FCT}^{\text{SRPT}}(f_0, l) + \sum_{f \in F_l} \Delta\text{FCT}^{\text{SRPT}}(f, l)$$

$$= \frac{1}{B_l} \left(s_{f_0} + \sum_{f \in F_l} \min(s_f, s_{f_0}) \right) = \text{FCT}^{\text{FAIR}}(f_0, l). \tag{4.9}$$

4.2.4 *Invariance Condition*

Although the predicted FCT varies for different network scheduling policies, we show that the optimal placement can be invariant under certain conditions. Specifically, we have shown that under SRPT scheduling, the alternative objective (4.2) reduces to the fair-sharing FCT of the newly arrived flow (see (4.9)), and under Fair/LAS scheduling, this objective is approximately twice of the fair-sharing FCT (see (4.6)). Since constant-factor scaling does not affect the selection of placement, these results imply that we can use the same objective function to place flows no matter whether the network performs Fair, LAS, or SRPT scheduling.

Proposition 4.1. *If the network performs Fair, LAS, or SRPT flow scheduling and each flow is small relative to the total load on each link, then the optimal placement that minimizes (4.2) is always the one that minimizes bottleneck fair-sharing FCT of the newly arrived flow (4.4).*

Remark: Surprisingly, we have shown that when the network schedules flows by LAS or SRPT, we should place flows to minimize their predicted FCTs under Fair scheduling in order to optimize the objective (4.2).

4.3 CCT Prediction for Coflow Scheduling

We now revise the above formulas for the case that the network schedules traffic at the level of coflow. We study the following policies applied to coflow scheduling, including FCFS [Dogar *et al.* (2014a)], Fair, LAS [Chowdhury and Stoica (2015)], and an extension of SRPT called *permutation scheduling* [Chowdhury *et al.* (2014)]. For a coflow c, let s_c denote its total size (in number of bytes), and $s_{c,l}$ denote the sum size of the individual flows in c that traverse link l. We show that the idea of computing FCT can be generalized to predict the performance of coflows.

We make the following assumptions: (i) all flows of a coflow have the same priority, and (ii) all flows of a coflow complete simultaneously. The first assumption is based on a principle adopted by state-of-art coflow schedulers [Dogar *et al.* (2014a); Chowdhury *et al.* (2014)] that flows within a coflow should progress together; the second assumption is based on a state-of-art coflow rate adaptation mechanism [Chowdhury *et al.* (2014)], which slows down all but the slowest flows in a coflow to match the completion time of the slowest flow so as to conserve bandwidth without increasing the CCT. In particular, assumption (ii) allows us to apply the same objective functions (4.1, 4.2) in placing coflows, with f (f_0) replaced by c (c_0), FCT replaced by CCT, and p_f replaced by p_c (denoting the set of links traversed by any flow of a coflow c). The computation of $\mathrm{CCT}(c, l)$ and $\Delta\mathrm{CCT}(c, l)$ is, however, different from their single-flow counterparts, and will be detailed below. We redefine F_l to be the set of coflows with at least one constituent flow traversing link l.

4.3.1   CCT under FCFS Scheduling

Under FCFS scheduling, each link will serve traffic from existing coflows before serving the newly arrived coflow, thus

$$\mathrm{CCT}^{\mathrm{FCFS}}(c_0, l) = \frac{1}{B_l}\left(s_{c_0,l} + \sum_{c\in F_l} s_{c,l}\right), \tag{4.10}$$

and $\Delta\mathrm{CCT}^{\mathrm{FCFS}}(c, l) \equiv 0$ for all $c \in F_l$.

4.3.2   CCT under Fair or LAS Scheduling

Under fair sharing or LAS scheduling, all coflows of size smaller than c_0 will have finished and all coflows of size larger than c_0 will have transmitted s_{c_0} bytes when coflow c_0 completes. Under assumption (ii), flows within a coflow make progress proportionally to their sizes, and thus when a coflow traversing link l finishes b bytes over all its constituent flows, $bs_{c,l}/s_c$ bytes must be transmitted over link l. Therefore, each coflow $c \in F_l$ introduces a load of $\min(s_c,\ s_{c_0})s_{c,l}/s_c$ on link l during the lifetime of coflow c_0 and vice versa. The above arguments imply that

$$\mathrm{CCT}^{\mathrm{FAIR}}(c_0, l) = \frac{1}{B_l}\left(s_{c_0,l} + \sum_{\substack{c\in F_l \\ s_c \le s_{c_0}}} s_{c,l} + \sum_{\substack{c\in F_l \\ s_c > s_{c_0}}} \frac{s_{c_0}s_{c,l}}{s_c} \right) \tag{4.11}$$

for the newly arrived coflow c_0, and

$$\Delta\mathrm{CCT}^{\mathrm{FAIR}}(c, l) = \frac{s_{c_0,l}}{B_l s_{c_0}}\min(s_c,\ s_{c_0}) \tag{4.12}$$

for each existing coflow $c \in F_l$. From the above, we see that

$$\sum_{c\in F_l}\Delta\mathrm{CCT}^{\mathrm{FAIR}}(c, l) = \frac{1}{B_l}\left(\sum_{\substack{c\in F_l \\ s_c \le s_{c_0}}} \frac{s_c s_{c_0,l}}{s_{c_0}} + \sum_{\substack{c\in F_l \\ s_c > s_{c_0}}} s_{c_0,l} \right), \tag{4.13}$$

which is different from (4.11) unless $s_{c,l}/s_c = s_{c_0,l}/s_{c_0}$ for all $c \in F_l$. It means that compared to the single-flow Fair/LAS scheduling, where minimizing the objective (4.2) reduces to minimizing the FCT of the newly arrived flow, we have to explicitly consider the impact on existing coflows through (4.13) (in addition to (4.11)) under coflow Fair/LAS scheduling.

4.3.3 *CCT under Permutation Scheduling*

Permutation scheduling [Chowdhury *et al.* (2014)] serves the coflows sequentially and includes many scheduling policies as special cases (e.g., FCFS and all variations of SRPT). Given a permutation $\pi = (\pi_c)_{c \in F_l \cup \{c_0\}}$ of all the coflows sharing link l, where π_c is the order of scheduling coflow c, the CCT of the newly arrived coflow c_0 equals

$$\mathrm{CCT}^\pi(c_0, l) = \frac{1}{B_l} \sum_{\pi_c \leq \pi_{c_0}} s_{c,l}, \tag{4.14}$$

and the increase in CCT for each existing coflow $c \in F_l$ equals

$$\Delta\mathrm{CCT}^\pi(c, l) = \frac{s_{c_0,l}}{B_l} \mathbb{1}_{\pi_c > \pi_{c_0}}, \tag{4.15}$$

which can be used to evaluate the first objective (4.1).

For the second objective (4.2), we have

$$\mathrm{CCT}^\pi(c_0, l) + \sum_{c \in F_l} \Delta\mathrm{CCT}^\pi(c, l)$$

$$= \frac{1}{B_l} \left(\sum_{\pi_c \leq \pi_{c_0}} s_{c,l} + s_{c_0,l} |\{c \in F_l : \pi_c > \pi_{c_0}\}| \right). \tag{4.16}$$

In particular, for a counterpart of SRPT called *smallesT-Coflow-First (TCF)* [Chowdhury *et al.* (2014)], (4.16) becomes

$$\mathrm{CCT}^{\mathrm{TCF}}(c_0, l) + \sum_{c \in F_l} \Delta\mathrm{CCT}^{\mathrm{TCF}}(c, l)$$

$$= \frac{1}{B_l} \left(s_{c_0,l} + \sum_{\substack{c \in F_l \\ s_c \leq s_{c_0}}} s_{c,l} + \sum_{\substack{c \in F_l \\ s_c > s_{c_0}}} s_{c_0,l} \right), \tag{4.17}$$

which is similar to the CCT under fair sharing (4.11) if $s_{c,l}/s_c = s_{c_0,l}/s_{c_0}$ for all $c \in F_l$, $s_c > s_{c_0}$.

4.3.4 *Invariance Condition*

The above analysis shows that in the special case of $s_{c,l}/s_c = s_{c_0,l}/s_{c_0}$ for all $c \in F_l$, i.e., all coflows split traffic among traversed links in the same way, the objective (4.2) satisfies $\mathrm{CCT}^{\mathrm{FAIR}}(c_0, l) + \sum_{c \in F_l} \Delta\mathrm{CCT}^{\mathrm{FAIR}}(c, l) \approx 2\mathrm{CCT}^{\mathrm{FAIR}}(c_0, l)$ under Fair/LAS scheduling (assuming $s_{c_0,l} \ll \sum_{c \in F_l\, s_c \leq s_{c_0}} s_{c,l} + \sum_{c \in F_l\, s_c > s_{c_0}} s_{c_0,l}$), and $\mathrm{CCT}^{\mathrm{TCF}}(c_0, l) +$

$\sum_{c \in F_l} \Delta \text{CCT}^{\text{TCF}}(c, l) = \text{CCT}^{\text{FAIR}}(c_0, l)$ under TCF scheduling. By arguments similar to Proposition 4.1, we have the following statement.

Proposition 4.2. *If the network performs Fair, LAS, or TCF coflow scheduling, each coflow imposes a small load on each link (relative to its total load), and $s_{c,l}/s_c$ are identical among all coflows $c \in F_l$ for each link l, then the optimal placement that minimizes (4.2) is always the one that minimizes the bottleneck fair-sharing CCT of the newly arrived coflow as predicted by (4.11).*

Remark: We note that compared to the case of flow scheduling (Proposition 4.1), the invariance property for coflow scheduling only holds in very special cases when all the coflows split traffic in the same way. It means that in contrast to flow placement, there is rarely a uniformly optimal placement for coflows under different coflow scheduling policies, and it is crucial to customize coflow placement according to the underlying coflow scheduling policy in the network.

4.4   NEAT Task Placement Framework

NEAT targets data-intensive applications such as MapReduce or directed acyclic graph DAG-based systems (such as Spark, Tez etc.). Such applications run in multiple stages and NEAT aims at placing tasks in each stage with the goal of minimizing the average completion time of all the active tasks in the system. For example, a MapReduce job has two stages, Map (where input data is processed) and Reduce (where results of Map stage are summarized) and each stage may have a data shuffle part and a data processing part. Both data shuffle and data processing contribute to the total completion time of a job. Similarly, DAG-based applications can be considered an extension of MapReduce applications, which can have multiple Map/Reduce phases [Jalaparti *et al.* (2015)]. Therefore, for simplicity, we use MapReduce as the base model and then extend it to DAG for multi-stage jobs.

4.4.1   *Flow Placement*

NEAT places a new task in two steps: First, it identifies a set of candidate hosts for task placement and next, it selects a best host among these for task execution.

1) *Identification of preferred hosts:* For a given task, NEAT divides nodes into *preferred* hosts and *non-preferred* hosts based on the the size of the current task and the node state (defined as the smallest remaining flow size on each node). If the task generates a flow of size s, then a node is a preferred host if it is idle or all the flows currently scheduled on this node are no smaller than s. Using preferred hosts provides various benefits. First, it reduces the communication overhead among the network daemons and task placement daemons. For each new task, the task daemon contacts only a subset of hosts to get predicted task completion times. Thus, it improves the time taken to search the right candidate such that the selection time is linear in the number of candidate hosts. Secondly, using preferred hosts compliments the benefits of different network scheduling policies. For example, under the Fair or LAS policy, it ensures that long flows are not placed with existing short flows (although short flows can be placed with existing long flows under LAS scheduling), thus improving separation between short and long flows and reducing the switch queuing delays experienced by the short flows. Similarly, under the SRPT policy, it makes sure that the new task can start data transfer immediately. The preferred hosts are further compared in the next step. If there is no preferred host, such that every node has at least one flow smaller than the flow of the current task, then this preference is ignored, i.e., all the nodes are considered preferred hosts. NEAT, in case of large set of preferred hosts, can also consider input data placement to limit the number of preferred hosts for each task.

2) *Selection of a best host:* Given a set of preferred hosts, the next step is to select a host that achieves the minimum task completion time. The *completion time* of a task depends on: i) the time required to transfer input data, and ii) the time required to process the data. The data transfer time is captured by the predicted FCT/CCT, which is obtained from the network daemon (see Section 3). The data processing time depends on the available node resources (e.g., CPU and memory), which can be obtained from an existing per-node resource manager (e.g., Hadoop node manager). In the current design, NEAT compares the available node resources of each preferred host with requirements imposed by the application (e.g., minimum CPU and memory) to identify candidate hosts, and then selects the one that gives the minimum data transfer time. However, this design can be easily extended with a processing time predictor to minimize the total task completion time; we leave the details to future work.

Remark: NEAT is an online scheduler that greedily optimizes the performance of each new task. We choose this design because: (i) it significantly simplifies the computation per placement, and (ii) it approximates the optimal placement under certain conditions as specified in Proposition 4.1 and 4.2. Note that NEAT only places each task once at the beginning of its lifetime, and does not move any task during its execution.

4.4.2   *Coflow Placement*

Compared to flow placement, coflow placement poses additional challenges. Ideally, we want to jointly place all the flows in a coflow to minimize the completion time of the slowest flow. However, in the case of one-to-many or many-to-many coflows, joint placement of all the flows in a coflow has exponential complexity due to the exponentially many possible solutions. To solve this problem, we use a sequential heuristic, where we first place the largest flow within the coflow using the flow placement algorithm, and then place the second largest flow using the same algorithm based on the updated network state, and so on. This sequential heuristic used for coflow placement should have quadratic complexity. The reason for placing flows in descending order of their sizes is that larger flows are more likely to be the critical flows determining the completion time of the coflow and hence should be placed on nodes that have more available resources. We leave evaluation of other coflow placement algorithms as a future work. Note that many-to-one coflows do not have the complexity problem and thus can be placed optimally.

4.4.3   *Application to MapReduce Scheduling*

NEAT considers each MapReduce job as a concatenation of two tasks, one for the Map stage and one for the Reduce stage. Since there are generally multiple Map "tasks" in a job[1], this requires NEAT to place two coflows, one many-to-many coflow for reading input data into Map tasks and one many-to-one coflow for shuffling intermediate results to Reduce task (or many-to-many if there are multiple Reduce tasks). In both the cases, NEAT strives to achieve data locality if possible (as a node with the input data will have zero FCT/CCT), and minimizes data transfer time otherwise. For example, for placing Map tasks, it can leverage the data placement policy of the cluster filesystem (such as HDFS in Apache Yarn). In HDFS, data is usually placed on multiple locations for fault tolerance and to provide better data locality. During Map task placement, NEAT can either place

---

[1] Note that NEAT defines "task" differently from the MapReduce framework.

task on the nodes that has the input data available or choose the nodes using it's placement heuristic.

4.4.4 *Application to DAG Scheduling*

DAG-style applications can be modelled as an extension of MapReduce applications, except that a DAG may have multiple shuffle stages. NEAT considers each stage of a DAG job as a separate task and places flows (coflows) within a task using the procedure discussed in sections 4.4.1 and 4.4.2. The placement algorithm used by NEAT encourages placing tasks of same job on nodes close to the input data.

4.5 NEAT Optimizations

NEAT needs the state of all the active flows in the network to make optimal task placement decisions, which can incur significant overhead at both the network daemons and the task placement daemon. To reduce the overhead, NEAT introduces two optimizations: (i) instead of keeping individual states of all the active flows, each network daemon only maintains a compressed state with a constant size, (ii) instead of contacting all the network daemons, the task placement daemon determines a subset of nodes as candidate hosts based on local information and only contacts the network daemons at the candidate hosts.

Compressed Flow State: Keeping the original flow state requires space that grows linearly with the number of active flows, which limits scalability of the network daemon (with respect to network load). NEAT addresses this issue by approximating the FCT/CCT prediction using a compressed flow state. Each network daemon compresses information of its local flows (coflows) by quantizing the flow sizes into a fixed number of bins and maintaining summary statistics (e.g., total size and number of flows) in each bin. Compared with the original flow state that keeps track of individual flows, this compressed state has a size that is determined by the number of bins, regardless of the number of flows in the network.

We refer to the set of active flows F_l on link l as the *flow state* of link l. The flow states of all the links form the overall flow state F of the network. Note that under FCFS, we can easily compress F_l by storing only the total load ($\sum_{c \in F_l} s_f$ for flow scheduling and $\sum_{c \in F_l} s_{c,l}$ for coflow scheduling), which suffices for FCT/CCT prediction. We thus focus on the other scheduling policies in the sequel.

For FCT prediction, our idea is to divide flows on each link into a finite number of bins $n = 1, \ldots, N$, where we keep the following parameters for each bin: the minimum and maximum flow size $(s_{l,n}^{(1)}, s_{l,n}^{(2)})$, the total flow size (in number of bytes) $b_{l,n}$, and the number of flows $c_{l,n}$. In essence, we compress a set of flow sizes into a histogram of flow sizes with flexible bin boundaries $(s_{l,n}^{(1)}, s_{l,n}^{(2)})$. Using the compressed flow state, we can approximate (4.4) by:

$$\text{FCT}^{\text{FAIR}}(f_0, l) \approx \frac{1}{B_l}\left(s_{f_0} + \sum_{n=1}^{p} b_{l,n} + s_{f_0} \sum_{n=p+1}^{N} c_{l,n}\right), \qquad (4.18)$$

where $p = m_l(s_{f_0})$ and $m_l(s) \in \{1, \ldots, N\}$ is the index of the bin containing flow size s (i.e., $s_{l,m_l(s)}^{(1)} \leq s < s_{l,m_l(s)}^{(2)}$). Other predictions in § 4.2 can be approximated similarly, although we only need to approximate (4.4) if the invariance condition in Proposition 4.1 is satisfied. Note that storing $b_{l,n}$ is optional as it can be approximated by $c_{l,n}s$ for some $s \in [s_{l,n}^{(1)}, s_{l,n}^{(2)})$.

For CCT prediction, the compressed flow state in each bin has two additional attributes: $d_{l,n}$, denoting the total load on link l (i.e., sum of $s_{c,l}$ over coflows in this bin), and $e_{l,n}$, denoting the total normalized load on link l (i.e., sum of $s_{c,l}/s_c$ over coflows in the bin). Assuming $q = m_l(s_{c_0})$, for Fair/LAS scheduling, we can approximate (4.11) by

$$\text{CCT}^{\text{FAIR}}(c_0, l) \approx \frac{1}{B_l}\left(s_{c_0,l} + \sum_{n=1}^{q} d_{l,n} + s_{c_0} \sum_{n=q+1}^{N} e_{l,n}\right), \qquad (4.19)$$

and (4.13) by

$$\sum_{c \in F_l} \Delta\text{CCT}^{\text{FAIR}}(c, l) \approx \frac{s_{c_0,l}}{B_l s_{c_0}}\left(\sum_{n=1}^{q} b_{l,n} + s_{c_0} \sum_{n=q+1}^{N} c_{l,n}\right). \qquad (4.20)$$

Under TCF scheduling, we can approximate the righthand side of (4.17) by

$$\frac{1}{B_l}\left(s_{c_0,l} + \sum_{n=1}^{q} d_{l,n} + s_{c_0,l} \sum_{n=q+1}^{N} c_{l,n}\right). \qquad (4.21)$$

Here storing $e_{l,n}$ is also optional as it can be approximated by $d_{l,n}/s$ for some $s \in [s_{l,n}^{(1)}, s_{l,n}^{(2)})$.

Remark: The compressed flow state has a size that is linear in the number of bins (which is a design parameter), regardless of the number of flows in the network. The cost of this compression is the loss of accuracy in the FCT/CCT prediction, caused by uncertainty in the sizes of flows (coflows) that are in the same bin as the newly arrived flow (coflow). The bin sizes can be set based on the datacenter traffic distribution. For example, for heavy tailed traffic [Alizadeh *et al.* (2011)], one can use exponentially growing bin sizes to have smaller bin sizes for short flows and large bin sizes for long flows.

Reduced Communication Overhead: NEAT uses distributed components (network daemons) spread across the network to maintain the flow states (see Figure 1.2). To minimize the communication overhead between the task placement daemon and the network daemons, the network daemons do not always report their updated flow states; instead, the task placement daemon pings the network daemons to get the predicted task performance when it needs to place a new task.

In a large cluster, the task placement daemon has to contact a large number of network daemons to place a task. To further reduce the overhead, the task placement daemon uses local information to reduce the number of network daemons it needs to contact. Specifically, it only contacts a network daemon if (i) the node it resides on is sufficiently close to the input data (e.g., in the same rack or a rack one-hop away from the input data), and (ii) if the node state (i.e., the smallest residual size of flows currently scheduled on this node) is no smaller than the size of the current task. Note that without contacting the network daemon, the task placement daemon does not know the current node state. In our design, the task placement daemon caches the node states previously reported by the network daemons and uses the cached values as estimates.

4.6   Evaluation

We evaluate NEAT using trace-driven simulations based on ns2 [ns2 (2006)] as well as experiments on a small-scale testbed.

4.6.1   *Simulation Settings*

Datacenter Topology: We use a 160 node, 3-tier multi-rooted topology for our evaluation comprising layers of ToR (Top-of-Rack) switches, aggregation switches and core switches, similar to [Al-Fares *et al.* (2008); Vamanan *et al.* (2012b); Wilson *et al.* (2011b)]. Each host-ToR link has a capacity of 1 Gbps whereas all other links are of 10 Gbps. The end-to-end round-trip propagation delay (in the absence of queuing) between hosts via the core switch is $300\mu s$.

Traffic Workloads: We consider traffic workloads that are derived from

Scheme	Parameters
DCTCP	qSize = 250 pkts
	markingThresh = 65
L^{2}DCT	minRTO = 10 msec
PASE	qSize = 250 pkts
	minRTO (flows in top queue) = 10 msec
	minRTO (flows in other queues) = 200 msec
	numQue = 8

patterns observed in production datacenters. We evaluate NEAT using the benchmark Hadoop (map-reduce)[Dean and Ghemawat (2008)] and web-search [Alizadeh *et al.* (2013b)] workloads. These workloads contain a diverse mix of short and long flows with a heavy-tailed flow size distribution. In the web-search workload, more than 75% of all bytes are from 50% of the flows with sizes in the range [1,20MB]. The hadoop workload is less skewed: ~50% of the flows are less than 100MB in size and 4% flows are larger than 80GB. Note that we always use these settings unless specified otherwise.

Protocols Compared: We compare NEAT with two task scheduling strategies: load aware placement (minLoad) and locality aware placement (minDist). We consider several state-of-art datacenter network scheduling strategies including DCTCP (that implements Fair) [Alizadeh *et al.* (2011)], L^{2}DCT (that implements LAS) [Munir *et al.* (2013c)], and PASE (that implements SRPT) [Munir *et al.* (2014)] for flow scheduling and Varys [Chowdhury *et al.* (2014)] for coflow scheduling. minLoad places each task on the node with the minimum network load, defined as the utilization ratio of its link to ToR. minDist places each task as close as possible to its input data, as proposed by earlier schemes [Jalaparti *et al.* (2015)]. We also test coflow performance using smallest coflow first (SCF) heuristic. We implemented DCTCP, L^{2}DCT, PASE, and Varys using the source code provided by the authors to evaluate their scheme. The parameters of these protocols are set according to the recommendations provided by the authors, or reflect the best settings, which we determined experimentally (see Table 4.1). For FCT prediction, we use Fair sharing based prediction model unless stated otherwise and for CCT prediction, we use the prediction models corresponding to each evaluated coflow scheduling.

Performance Metrics: We consider the average flow completion time (AFCT) for the flow-based scheduling and coflow completion time (CCT) for coflow-based scheduling schemes. We use *gap from optimal* as the performance metric. For example, for FCT based schemes, the gap from optimal is calculated as $(FCT - FCT^{opt})/FCT^{opt}$, where FCT^{opt} is the optimal FCT defined as the time it takes to complete the data transfer when that is the only flow (coflow) in the network. Note that the gap from optimal equals slowdown (a.k.a. stretch) minus one. The gap from optimal tells us the margin for performance improvement for different kind of network scheduling policies. For example, we observe in our evaluation that the room for improvement is more for suboptimal scheduling policies, in terms of FCT, (such as FAIR, LAS) and less for near-optimal network scheduling policies (such as SRPT).

4.7 Macrobenchmarks

NEAT improves application performance upto 3.7x, compared to the existing task placement algorithms that only consider data and compute, by incorporating network state and network scheduling policies into task placement decisions. Below, we first discuss NEAT performance in placing flows and then its performance in placing coflows.

Flow placement performance under Fair sharing: Figure 4.2 shows that NEAT outperforms minLoad and minDist by up to 3.6x for web-search workload and up to 3.7x for Hadoop workloads when the network employs Fair sharing scheduling policy. This is because NEAT chooses the node with minFCT to finish flows faster and uses node state NEAT to avoid placing short flows on same links with long flows. Note that many of the existing policies deployed in the datacenter employ Fair sharing discipline. This shows that even if datacenter does not implement any optimized network scheduling mechanism, NEAT can improve application performance significantly by being aware of network state.

Flow placement performance under different network scheduling policies: Figure 4.3 shows NEAT performance for Hadoop workload when the network uses L^2DCT (LAS) and PASE (SRPT) as network scheduling policies. NEAT improves the performance by 2.7x compared to minLoad and by upto 3.2x compared to minDist when used with L^2DCT. NEAT also improves the performance by 30% compared to minLoad and by upto 20% compared to minDist when used with PASE. Note that PASE is a near-optimal algorithm and there is very little performance improvement margin for NEAT. Also, observe that minDist and minLoad perform differently under different scheduling policies, whereas, NEAT consistently performs better than both for all the evaluated network scheduling policies. We

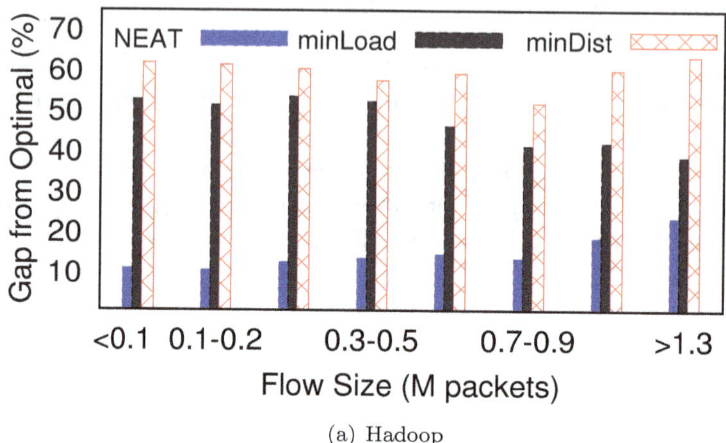

(a) Hadoop

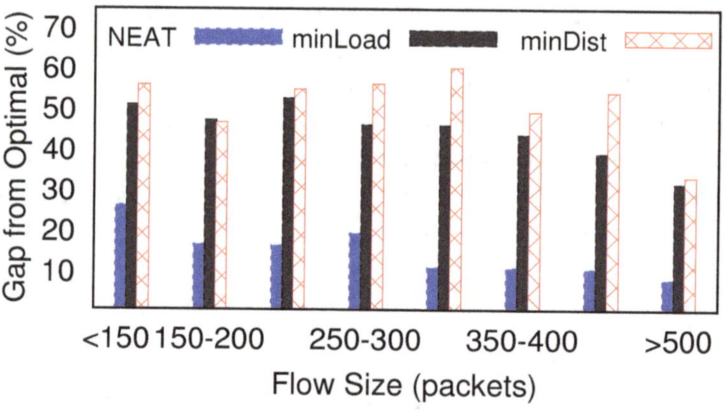

(b) Websearch

Fig. 4.2   Flow placement under DCTCP

observe similar performance trends with websearch workloads.

CoFlow placement performance under different network scheduling policies: NEAT improves the CCT performance for Hadoop workloads by upto 25% for two coflow scheduling policies, 1) Varys (Figure 4.4(a)) and 2) Smallest Coflow First (SCF) (Figure 4.4(b)). Coflow placement requires a group of flows to be placed in a batch. For coflow placement, NEAT works as described in Section 5.1, while minLoad and minDist are modified as follows - For minLoad, we place each flow of the coflow separately, in the decreasing order of flow sizes, on a node that has the minimum network

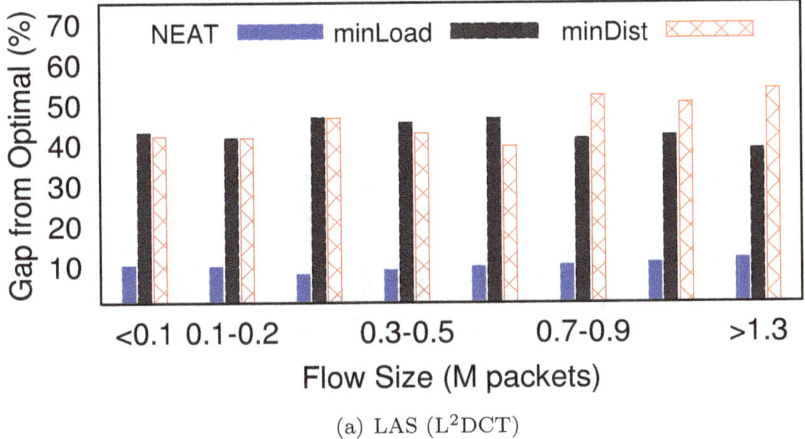

(a) LAS (L^{2}DCT)

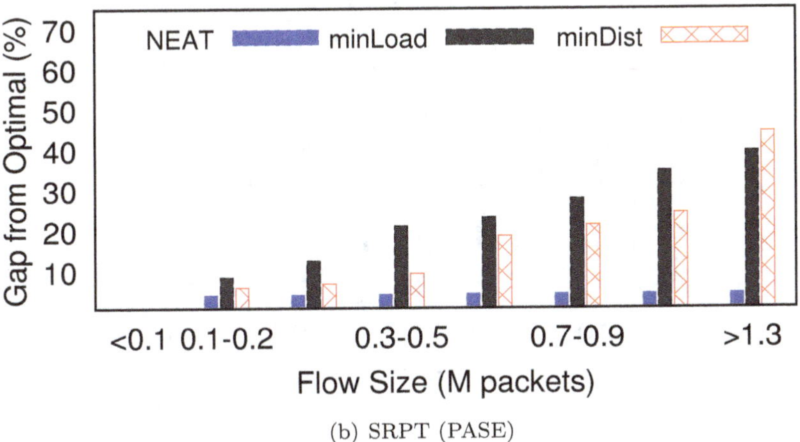

(b) SRPT (PASE)

Fig. 4.3 Flow placement under Hadoop workload

load. For minDist, our goal is to place flows of the same coflow within the same rack and close to input data and we start by placing the largest flow of a coflow first. NEAT performs better under both coflow scheduling policies, however its gains are limited by the performance of underlying coflow scheduling policy. For example, minDist with Varys scheduling performs better than NEAT with SCF scheduling. The reason for this is that Varys, which adjusts the flow rates based on the smallest bottleneck heuristic, is a much better heuristic than SCF. However, we observe that the gap from

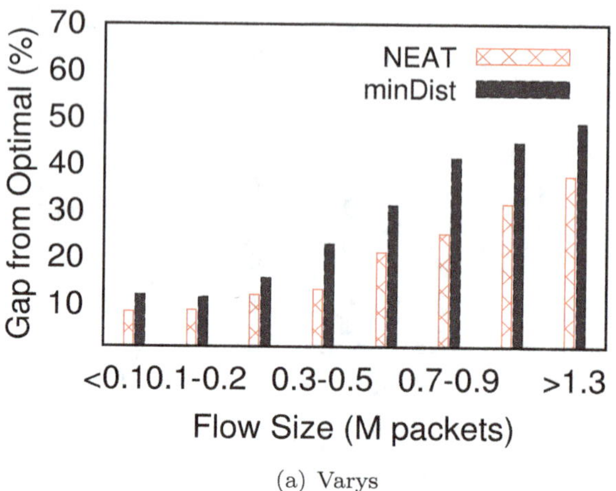

(a) Varys

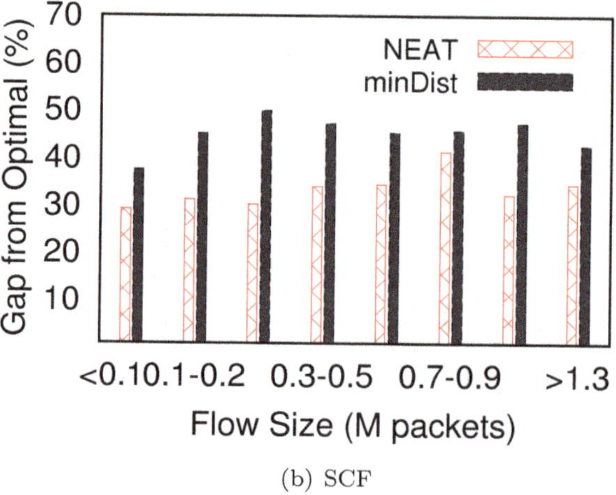

(b) SCF

Fig. 4.4   CoFlow placement for Hadoop workload

optimal is substantial (30% to 50%), for these strategies, for large flow sizes with Varys and nearly for all flow sizes with SCF. The reason for this gap is that the optimal completion time is not always achievable, even under the optimal scheduling, as our definition of optimal ignores resource competition from other flows/coflows. Also, many of these protocols implement certain approximations, instead of the actual optimal scheduling algorithm, to be more deployment friendly.

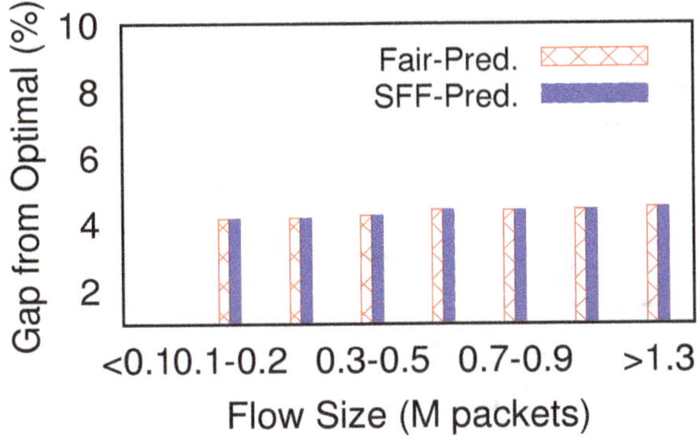

Fig. 4.5   Fair prediction vs SRPT prediction

4.8   Microbenchmarks

In this section, we discuss various aspects of NEAT design, with the help of several micro-benchmarks. We analyze NEAT dynamics using Hadoop workload under SRPT (PASE) network scheduling policy, unless stated otherwise. Our evaluation shows that NEAT optimizations (such as prediction assuming FAIR policy only, preferred hosts) improve the application performance and it can predict task completion times quite accurately.

Benefits of using Fair predictor: Figure 4.5 shows the NEAT performance when task completion time is predicted using the Fair-sharing model (Eq. 4.4) or the SRPT-sharing model (Eq. 4.7) when the underlying network scheduling mechanism is SRPT. Both predictors achieve similar performance, therefore, even though the network performs SRPT flow scheduling, NEAT can perform FCT prediction by assuming the fair-sharing principle. This validates our proposition, in §4.2.4, which states that for flow based network scheduling mechanisms, task placement using minimum predicted task completion time, assuming FAIR predictor, can provide better performance for any flow based network scheduling policy.

Benefits of using preferred hosts aware placement: Figure 4.6 shows the benefits of using preferred hosts for making task placement decisions. To evaluate the impact on performance, we compare NEAT performance to minFCT. minFCT strategy makes task placement decision based on the predicted task completion times alone and ignores the node states i.e., it places each task on to a node with the smallest predicted FCT and does not consider the priority of the tasks already scheduled on that node. Fig-

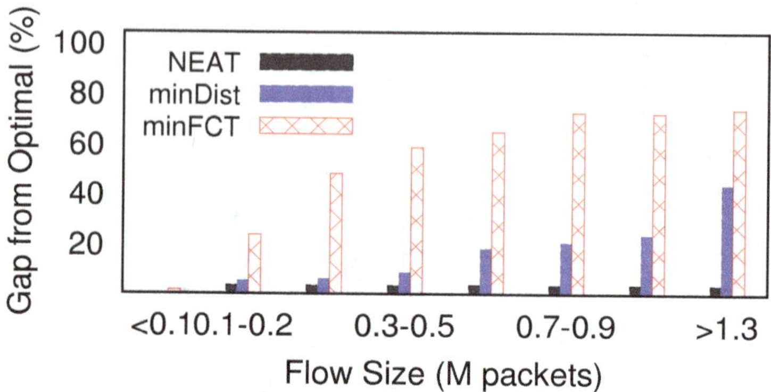

Fig. 4.6   Benefits of using preferred hosts placement

ure 4.6 shows that minFCT placement degrades application performance by up to 50%, and performs even worse than minDist placement. NEAT on the other hand achieves better performance by being aware of node states. Intuitively, minFCT hurts performance in two ways: i) it groups short flows together, thus increasing fair sharing among short flows. ii) for long flows it selects nodes with many short flows, thus long flows experience more preemption by the currently scheduled and newly arriving short flows. We note that the comparison between minFCT and minDist is workload-dependent, e.g., for the workloads, where short and long flows have proportional number of bytes, minFCT performs similar to or better than minDist placement. Thus, using preferred hosts based task placement not only minimizes communication overhead, but it also improves application performance.

Flow completion time prediction accuracy: NEAT can predict flow completion times with reasonable accuracy as shown in Figure 4.7. NEAT performance depends on accurately predicting completion times. It is important to keep the prediction error small because NEAT only considers currently active tasks while predicting FCTs and future task arrivals may make current placement decisions suboptimal. Figure 4.7 reports the prediction accuracy, which is calculated as $(FCT^{flow} - FCT^{pred})/FCT^{pred}$, where FCT^{flow} is the actual FCT and FCT^{pred} is the FCT predicted by NEAT. Figure 4.7 shows the prediction accuracy for short flows (Figure 4.7(a)), and long flows (Figure 4.7(b)) and we observe that the prediction error increases with the flow size. This is because, with the increase in flow size, the flow spends more time in the network and is affected more

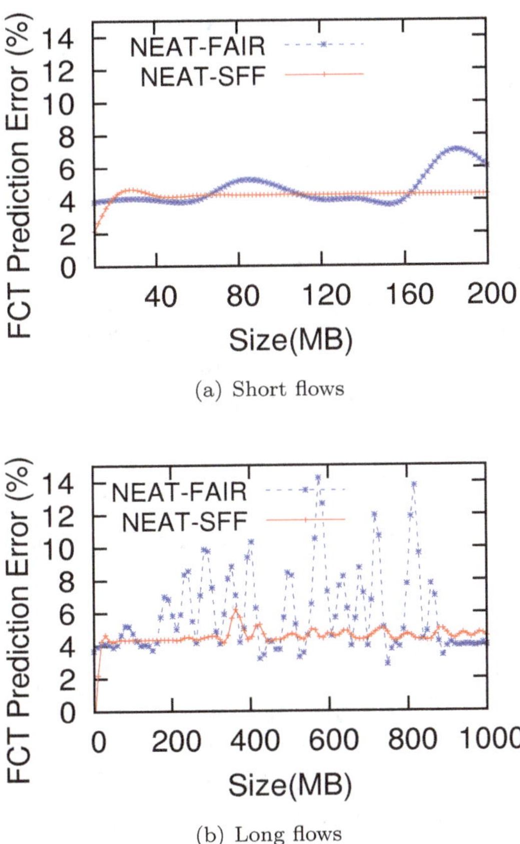

(a) Short flows

(b) Long flows

Fig. 4.7   Completion time prediction error

by the tasks arriving later in time. In many practical datacenter applications, most tasks generate short flows, for which NEAT can predict the FCT within 5% error. This experiment shows that NEAT is not very sensitive to mis-prediction in task completion time estimate and it is able to achieve good performance even in the presence of small inaccuracies in task completion time estimates.

4.9   Testbed Evaluation

We discuss testbed implementation and evaluation results.

Implementation: NEAT follows a master/slave architecture similar to Hadoop-Yarn [had (2006)], and we implement NEAT in Scala using support from Akka for messaging between task placement daemon (TD) and network daemons (ND). We currently implement NEAT as an application layer program by extending Varys implementation [Chowdhury *et al.* (2014)] and leave the integration with Hadoop-Yarn as a future work. Similar to Yarn, the TD acts as the resource manager (RM) and makes task placement decisions, and NDs act as node managers, which maintain flow state of the active jobs and share the network state upon receiving requests from the task placement daemon. The TD accepts a user job similar to RM and invokes network daemon APIs at the nodes (endhosts). Cluster framework (e.g., Spark or Hadoop) drivers can submit a job using the `register()` API to interact with NEAT. Upon receiving a request from the TD, NDs update their local states and reply with predicted task performance and node state. The TD then runs our placement algorithm to schedule flows on selected nodes. To support multiple network scheduling policies, we reuse Varys' `put()` and `get()` method to send and receive data between different nodes. Cluster frameworks can use NEAT `InputStream` and `OutputStream` to leverage various network scheduling policies. The desired network scheduling policy can be specified during network configuration phase.

Evaluation Results: We evaluate NEAT using a 10-node single-rack cluster consisting of DELL servers (with 1G NICs) and PICA-8 Gigabit switch with ECN support enabled. We consider scenario with all-to-all traffic based on Hadoop workload [Dean and Ghemawat (2008)] and generate traffic such that the average network load is 50%. We first generate the traffic using ns2 and replay the same traffic in the testbed. The hadoop workload generates many long flows as ~50% of the flows are less than 100MB in size and 4% flows are larger than 80GB. We compare NEAT to minLoad task placement under Fair (implemented by DCTCP) and LAS (implemented by L^2DCT) network scheduling policies. Because of the small scale of the testbed, we do not compare with minDist (since all node pairs have the same distance), and only evaluate using flow-based network scheduling policies.

Our evaluation shows that, compared to minLoad, NEAT can improve application performance by upto 30% under Fair scheduling and upto 27% under LAS scheduling policy, see Figure 4.8. The gain in testbed scenario is much less than the large scale simulations, and the reason for small gain is the small scale of the testbed. In our evaluation, we observe that a lot of long flows are generated that run simultaneously in the network and share links with short flows. Both the placement algorithms spread large flows across all the nodes in the network, over the time, and therefore increase the completion time of short flows because they share the network links

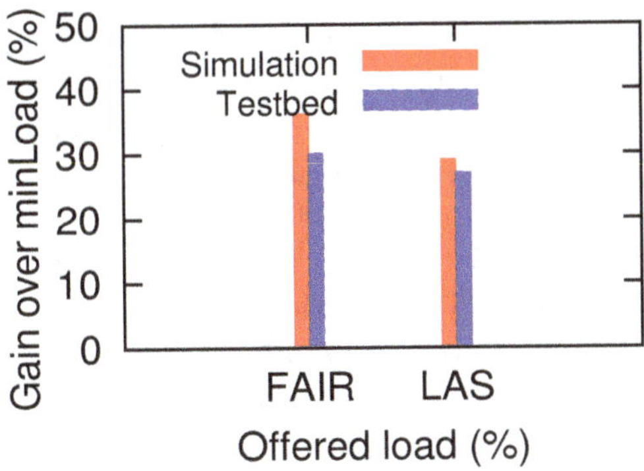

Fig. 4.8   Testbed: minLoad vs NEAT

and switch buffers, most of which are occupied by long flows. This effect is not observed in large scale networks where a flow can mostly have many available nodes to chose from. Although, the size of the testbed limits the amount of improvement, NEAT is able to improve the performance under both the network scheduling policies by making better placement decisions. We also compare testbed results to ns2 simulations using same settings as testbed setup and observe similar performance gains.

4.10   Discussion

Input Data Placement: NEAT can leverage the knowledge of input data locations to improve scalability and make more accurate placement decisions. However, input data may not be optimally placed, which limits the performance of NEAT. In such cases, NEAT can be combined with strategies like corral [Jalaparti *et al.* (2015)] to make input data and task placement decisions based on the task execution history.

Flow Size Information: NEAT requires flow size information to predict task performance, however, flow size may not always be available. For example, the motivation behind using LAS-based network scheduling is to address this challenge [Munir *et al.* (2013c)]. In such scenarios, NEAT can use approximate flow sizes based on the task execution history for performance prediction, as we have shown that NEAT minimizes task completion time even with some inaccuracy in predicted task completion times (§4.8). We leave evaluation of such scenarios for future work.

Generalization of Network Topologies: Currently, NEAT assumes a single-switch topology and predicts task performance based on the edge links only, however, any link in the network can be bottleneck in other topologies. To make better placement decisions, one can use a distributed state maintenance mechanism similar to PASE [Munir *et al.* (2014)] where a dedicated arbitrator maintains flow state for each link in the network. NEAT can choose the destination that gives the minimum completion time along the path from source to destination. Nevertheless, our evaluation shows that the single-switch abstraction already provides substantial performance improvement over existing solutions.

NEAT Scalability: NEAT introduces several optimizations to make system more scalable. For example, to mitigate the communication overhead among daemons, it uses node states while contacting nodes for performance prediction estimate. This reduces the amount of overhead messages sent over the network for communication among network and task placement daemons. Also, to reduce the overhead of task state maintenance by the network daemons, NEAT uses compressed flow state while predicting the task performance. As shown in §4.8, these optimizations help improve NEAT performance, however, we leave large scale scalability analysis of these optimizations as a future work.

4.11   Conclusion

This chapter discussed a task placement framework that takes into account the network scheduling policy and shows that significant performance gains can be obtained over task schedulers oblivious to network scheduling. NEAT task scheduler makes task placement decisions by using a pluggable task performance predictor that predicts the data transfer time of a given task under given network conditions and network scheduling policy. Despite several simplifying assumptions, NEAT achieves promising performance improvement under several commonly used network scheduling policies. Its pluggable architecture allows easy incorporation of sophisticated resource and application models.

Chapter 5

Bandwidth Allocation in Multi-tenant Datacenters

In this chapter, we discuss the design of a Stacked Congestion Control (SCC), which is a distributed host-based bandwidth allocation framework for multi-tenant datacenter networks. SCC can support both *performance isolation* and *objective scheduling*, and is readily-deployable. SCC has two layers to perform congestion control: (i) an underlay congestion control (UCC) layer handles contention among divisions (*i.e.* performance isolation), and (ii) a private congestion control (PCC) layer for each division to optimize its performance objective (*i.e.* objective scheduling).

SCC adds a shim layer at each endhost, that manages the bandwidth assigned to each objective-tenant tunnel at that endhost. In SCC, shim layer achieves bandwidth sharing among tunnels in two steps. First, it distributes resources among tunnels based on network weights and bandwidth requested from the tunnel. Next, it schedules flows inside the tunnel to optimize the objective performance. Each tunnel computes it's bandwidth requirement by taking into account the objective application type, flow characteristics, and network congestion. Each tunnel then contacts the shim layer with the request for the required bandwidth and the shim layer responds with the response bandwidth. To compute the response bandwidth, shim layer first satisfies the demands of all the flows, and then shares the available capacity among tunnels based on the network weights. Upon receiving the response bandwidth, the tunnel schedules its flows to maximize the gains of each application objective.

5.1 Underlay Congestion Control

Congestion Signal: UCC uses ECN as the congestion signal and uses weighted network sharing algorithms to derive the contemporary tunnel rate. At a high level SCC uses tunnels to perform congestion control. Each tunnel has a rate-limiting queue at it's ingress port in the endhost. A tunnel weight W_t is attached with each tunnel that determines the share of network bandwidth. For all outgoing packets in a tunnel, the ECN-enable bits in IP headers are set by the tunnel. In the receiver end of the tunnel, the ECN mark ratio is recorded; the destination host periodically sends ECN feedback; for all incoming TCP acknowledgement packets, ECN bit is removed before transferring to upper transport protocols. Note that if the upper transport protocol supports ECN, UCC should pass this information to PCC layer.

Tunnel Rate: SCC provides the tunnel with a bandwidth share that is proportional to its weight; This allocation is an end-to-end and work-conserving design. Each tunnel has a rate limiting queue attached to the ingress port in the source host. Based on the ECN feedback, each tunnel estimates the available bandwidth and adjusts the rate of the send queue. Similar to Seawall, we mimic the DCTCP behaviour in tunnel level congestion control. If there is no congestion in the network, the rate R_t increases as:

$$R_t = (1 + W_t) * R_t, \tag{5.1}$$

where, W_t is the weight assigned to a tunnel. Upon detecting congestion, the rate reduces as:

$$R_t = (1 - \alpha * W_t) * R_t, \tag{5.2}$$

where α is the level of congestion in the network.

Scaling Tunnel Weight: As a distributed solution, each tunnel in SCC, periodically generates its reference tunnel weight W_t' according to its PCC layer algorithm. This calculation is objective-oriented, and the corresponding algorithms are presented in Section 5.3. All tunnels in the same division should ensure that the global weight W_d allocated to this division is respected, by cooperatively scaling each tunnel's self-derived reference network weight.

A tracker is elected from all the source hosts in each division, and each source host periodically sends W_t' to this tracker. A scale factor are calculated as:

$$\lambda_d = W_d / \sum_{\forall t \in d} W_t', \tag{5.3}$$

and λ_d is periodically sent back to hosts in the division. Accordingly, each source hosts derive its contemporary weight value as follows:

$$W_t = \lambda_d * W_t'. \tag{5.4}$$

In this way, the division weight is dynamically divided among all its constituent tunnels. An example data path is shown in Figure 5.1. There are two completion time sensitive (CS) tunnels and one deadline sensitive (DS) tunnel among three pairs of hosts: division 1 contains two CS tunnels; division 2 contains one DS tunnel; all CS/DS flow(s) enter the CS/DS tunnel(s). As shown by the example in Figure 5.1, the sum of weights for CS tunnel 1 and tunnel 2 equals 3, which is equal to the division 2's allocated weight.

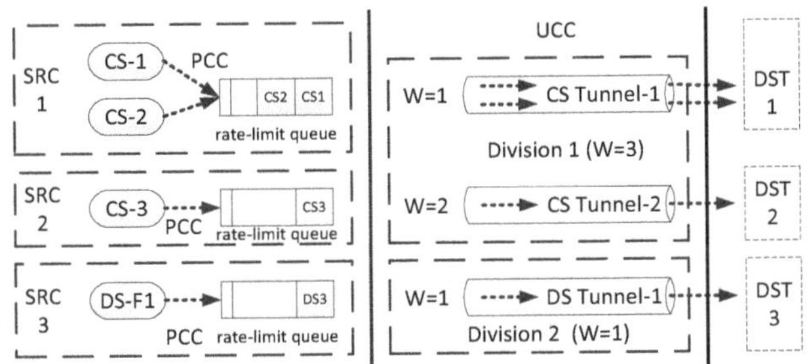

Fig. 5.1 SCC framework with tenant-objective tunnel abstraction.

Due to the impact of load balancing, in each tier of the network, the share of bandwidth obtained by a tunnel is statistically proportional to its weight. Since the sum of their weights equals the global weight allocated to this division, the division's bandwidth share is achieved.

5.2 Private Congestion Control

Congestion Signal: SCC is completely transparent to the upper layer transport protocols. The congestion signal for objective-oriented scheduling is generated from the underlying host send queue instead of the network. Each division tunnel has full control of using its own congestion signal and control law; it can either rely on existing objective-oriented transport protocols, or directly schedule flows in the tunnel. The upper transport protocols may enable ECN support, such as in D^2TCP, DCTCP and L^2DCT. Note that in SCC, ECN bits are used for division-level congestion control and before handing over to upper layers, all ECN marks are removed. For this scenario, SCC remarks the ECN bit based on concurrent queue length and properties of flows inside the tunnel. Otherwise, if the transport protocols rely on packet drop, a queue length should be set (*e.g.*, 100 packets).

Generate Reference Tunnel Weight and In-Tunnel Scheduling: To optimize the performance objective, there are two algorithm options for a particular division: (i) generate reference tunnel weight W_t' according to contained flows, and relies on upper layer transport protocols to schedule flows inside the tunnel; and (ii) integrated design of both reference tunnel weight and in-tunnel scheduling. We present our PCC algorithms in Section 5.3. Note that SCC is a general architecture: researchers can developed algorithms for different objectives, or algorithms also target LS/DS/CS flows but with better performance.

5.3 PCC Tunnel Algorithms

In this section, our designs of tunnel algorithms, for DS/CS/LS divisions are presented. To optimize the performance objective, we adopt an integrated design method of both reference tunnel weight and in-tunnel scheduling. Even if upper layer transport protocols are preferred to schedule flows inside the tunnel, the reference tunnel weight algorithms can still be used.

A goal of algorithms is that, for a division, using a datacenter network exclusively, the control mechanism should achieve comparable performance with and without SCC. Assume four DS flows with the flow priority $f_1 > f_2 > f_3 > f_4$; f_1 and f_2 share the same tunnel, and f_3 and f_4 share the same tunnel. Prior to SCC, and without the concern of coexistence, all DS flows may compete independently. With SCC , now f_1/f_2 tunnel competes with another tunnel that contains f_3/f_4. This metric reflects the overhead/gain of SCC algorithms.

The symbols used are listed in Table 5.1.

$M_s(t)$	remaining data size for session s at time t
$\delta_s(t)$	remaining time till deadline for session s at time t
$x_s(t)$	requested source rate for session s at time t
$Q_s(t)$	buffer status for session s at time t
λ_s	average data arrival rate for session s
Q_s^*	target average queue length
$BW_{req}(t)$	request from the host on the bandwidth at time t
$BW_{res}(t)$	response from the coordinator on thebandwidth at time t
τ	decision slot duration

5.3.1 *Deadline-Sensitive Tunnel*

Deadline-sensitive flows require to transfer a flow of certain size within a deadline. It is well known that for a single flow session s with remaining size M_s and deadline δ_s, a guaranteed bandwidth x_s no less than M_s/δ_s can meet its deadline. Therefore, SCC dynamically updates the required minimum bandwidth of each DS tunnel based on the sizes and deadlines of all active flows in the tunnel (step 1 and 2, Algo. 5.3.1). This requirement is updated periodically ($\approx$ msec).

Algorithm 3 Rate Control for DS Tunnel

At the beginning of each decision slot, the tunnel
Step 1: Updates the flow information, $\{M_s(t), \delta_s(t)\}$
Step 2: Estimates the rates $x_s^*(t) = \frac{M_s(t)}{\delta_s(t)}$ and $BW_{req}(t) = \sum_s x_s^*(t)$.
Step 3: Let $W_t' = BW_{req}(t)$, gets W_t from W_t', and set $BW_{res}(t) = W_t$.
In-tunnel scheduling

The tunnel responds to the allowed bandwidth, which may or may not be equal to the required bandwidth (step 3, Algo. 5.3.1). SCC can choose to either use or not use in-tunnel scheduling algorithm, irrespective of the upper layer transport protocols, . We demonstrate later in evaluation, that in-tunnel scheduling can provide significant performance improvement, which accredits to the flexibility of the SCC framework. This is because, while for a group of deadline-sensitive flows in the same connection, simply adding their minimum bandwidth requirement together may not be optimal, which can unnecessarily increase demanded bandwidth. Even worse, DS flows come and go; as a result, the derived bandwidth guarantee value should also be dynamic to keep up. Once a bandwidth is assigned by the coordinator, it satisfies as many deadline flows as possible, based on the EDF principle (step 4, Algo. 5.3.1). This not only serves existing flows, but new coming flows are also accommodated automatically.

5.3.2 *Completion-Sensitive Tunnel*

The bandwidth sharing mechanism for CS tunnels is similar to the DS tunnels, except that only flow sizes are used to compute required bandwidth. To mimic the Shortest-Flow-First (SFF) strategy, the inversion of flow size is used as each flow's weight (step 2, Algo. 5.3.2). Inside the CS tunnel, flows are simply scheduled by SFF.

Algorithm 4 Rate Control for CS Tunnel

At the beginning of each decision slot, the tunnel
Step 1: Updates the flow information, $\{M_s(t)\}$
Step 2: Estimates the weight $W_t' = \sum_s 1/M_s(t)$.
Step 3: Gets W_t from W_t'.
In-tunnel scheduling
Shortest-Flow-First

5.3.3 *Latency-Sensitive Tunnel*

For LS tunnels, the buffer length in the host/network queues defines the flow latency. This algorithm considers queuing at the end-hosts only, not from the switches in the network. We rely on tunnel level UCC protocols to maintain switch queues at a low-level, and an additional option is to put LS flows into a higher physical queue.

SCC maintains small queues in the tunnel by using ECN based notification. To compute bandwidth requirement, PCC leverages insights from how existing transport protocols work. For example, most of the existing datacenter transport protocols start with initial congestion window of 10 packets (such as DCTCP, L^{2}DCT, etc.,), and to avoid timeouts, they need at least one ACK per RTT. Therefore, we set average bandwidth of a tunnel to be at least $10 \times N_f$, where N_f is the number of LS flows in each tunnel. Additionally, we also consider the queue size to determine the target rate for the LS flows as listed in Algo. 5.3.3.

Algorithm 5 Rate Control for LS Tunnel

At the beginning of each decision slot, the tunnel
Step 1: Update the current queue status $\{Q_s(t)\}$
Step 2: Estimates the rates $x_s^*(t) = \frac{Q_s(t) - \epsilon_s Q_s^*}{\tau} \mathbf{1}\left[Q_s(t) > \epsilon_s Q_s^*\right]$ and $BW_{req}(t) = \sum_s x_s^*(t)$.
Step 3: Let $W_t' = BW_{req}(t)$, gets W_t from W_t', and set $BW_{res}(t) = W_t$.
In-tunnel scheduling
Shortest-Flow-First

5.4 Testbed Verification

In this section, we first discuss SCC system implementation and testbed evaluation. Then, we compare simulation results to testbed results.

System Implementation: We implement the SCC shim layer as a Netfilter kernel module in Linux. Two hash based flow tables, one for send and one for receive, are used for packet classification and for tracking per-flow state. To enforce accurate rates over short timescales, we use Linux high-resolution kernel timer, HRTIMER, for our rate limiters.

At the sender, we use the LOCAL_OUT hook to intercept all outgoing packets to enforce virtual tunnel abstraction. Each outgoing packet is first matched against the send table and then encapsulated using pipe-level IP/UDP header encapsulation. To support ECN, the ECN-capable (ECT) codepoint is marked in every packet's IP header. The packet is then forwarded to a rate limited per-tunnel queue.

At the receiver end, we use the LOCAL_IN hook to intercept all incoming packets. Each packet is matched against the receive table, and its ECN bit is checked. The receiver shim layer calculates the fraction of ECN marking packets and delivers this information back to the sender that uses it to perform tunnel-level congestion control. We have not implemented in-tunnel algorithms for the testbed.

Testbed Experiments: For Testbed experiments, we use a single rack with 16 DELL servers (with 1G NICs) and PICA-8 Gigabit switch with ECN support enabled. For evaluation, we consider three kind of traffic, latency-sensitive (DCTCP), deadline-sensitive (D^2TCP) and completion-sensitive (L^2DCT). We use same settings as Base-DS, Base-LS and Base-CS for each traffic.

First, we consider CS application in isolation, with and without SCC support. Flows are generated such that it incurs an average load of 400 Mbps (low load). Figure 5.2(a) (*i.e.* only scenario) shows that performance of CS flows remain the same with or without SCC support in this scenario. The reason is that, in a network with low load, flows do not experience interference and finish quickly.

Next, we consider coexistence of CS/DS (medium load) and CS/DS/LS (high load) flows in the network. With SCC support enabled (Figure 5.2(a)), the AFCT of L^2DCT flows is improved by 17%, 53% for CS/DS and CS/DS/LS coexistence scenarios, respectively. With SCC, deadline missing of DS flows is reduced by 2×, 1× for CS/DS and CS/DS/LS coexistence scenario, respectively.

Verification using Simulations: In this section, we verify NS2 simulations via testbed results, when the CS and DS flows coexist in the network, under the motivation example scenario. We use same settings as Base-DS, and Base-CS for each application and vary network load. In this scenario,

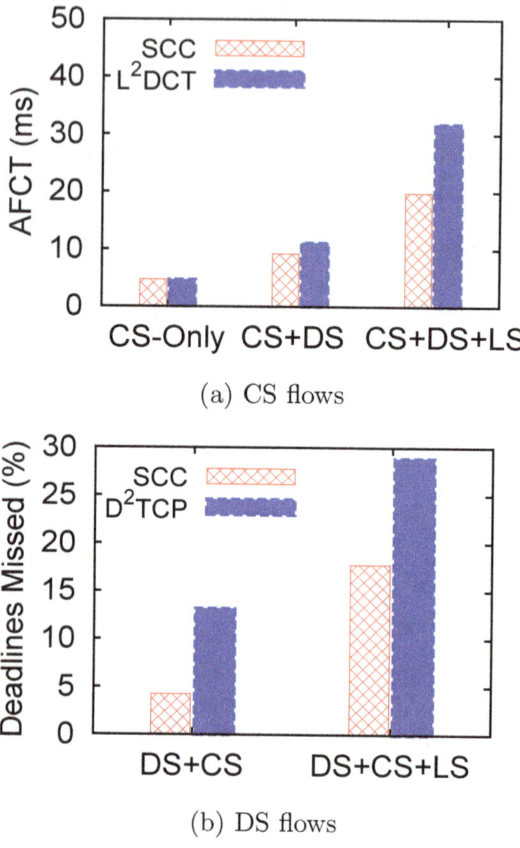

(a) CS flows

(b) DS flows

Fig. 5.2   Testbed Results w/ & w/o SCC.

as shown earlier, DS flows and CS flows experience degraded performance (Fig. 2.5(c) and (d)). Figure 5.3 shows that with SCC support, fewer flows miss their deadlines, more specifically, at higher loads, we observe $4\times$ performance improvement compared to when D^2TCP is used. Similarly, completion time of flows is improved by 5x at higher loads. This is due to the in-queueing at the end-hosts and the adaptive ECN marking at shim layer. We observe similar performance trends as testbed at low and medium loads, while simulations show better improvement at higher loads.

5.5   Large-scale NS-2 Simulations

Our evaluation addresses the following questions:

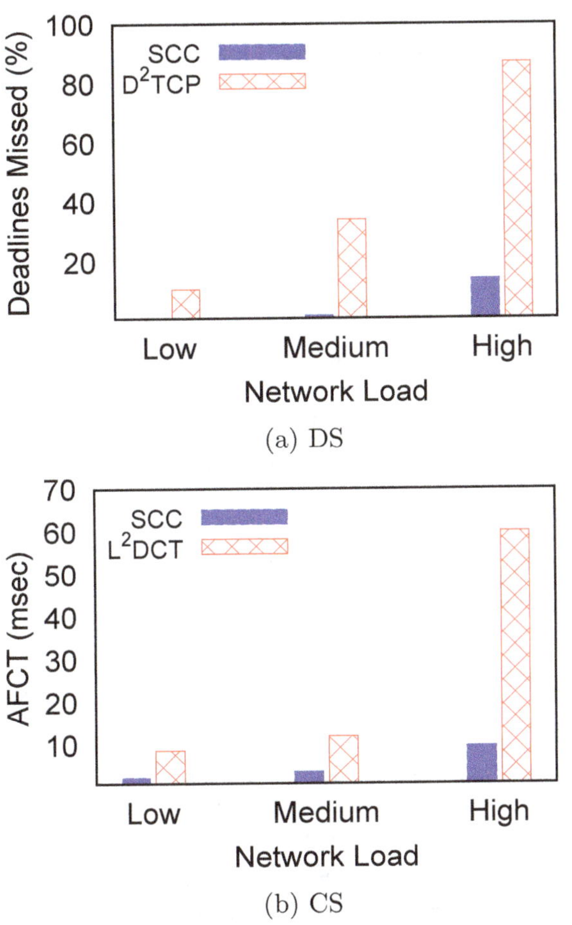

(a) DS

(b) CS

Fig. 5.3 Performance under CS/DS coexistence scenario

(1) **Can SCC improve the performance of different flows when they coexist?** We evaluate the scenarios where flows with different performance objectives coexist in the data center network. SCC is able to meet the requirements of objectives like CS, DS or LS simultaneously across a wide range of workloads such as Web-search [Alizadeh *et al.* (2011)], Data-mining [Greenberg *et al.* (2009)] and MapReduce [Chen *et al.* (2011)]. SCC improves performance by up to 3.2× for DS flows and 40% for CS flows as compared to state-of-art protocols like pFabric [Alizadeh *et al.* (2013b)].

(2) **Can SCC achieve the same or even better performance when**

only flows of the same objective exist in the network? In our evaluation, we show that SCC can achieve similar or better performance for protocols when they exist in the network alone. At high loads, SCC can reduce the deadline miss rate by up to 2× and achieve similar AFCTs.

(3) **Does SCC consistently perform well?** We test SCC performance in oversubscribed settings and with different transport protocols. The results demonstrate that with SCC enabled, most protocols deliver better performance.

Evaluation Setup: We use a Clos topology for NS2 simulations, unless specified otherwise. The capacity of edge links is 1 Gbps and core links is 10 Gbps. We assume ECN capable switches with 250 KB buffering and maximum end-to-end RTT of 300 usec [Munir *et al.* (2014)].

We model two traffic classes. Class-I traffic belongs to deadline-sensitive small message application and requires deadline guarantees. Class II traffic is similar to Class-I, but has different objective than deadline, such as minimizing flow completion times or latency-guarantees. We replicate Web-search [Alizadeh *et al.* (2011)], Data-mining [Greenberg *et al.* (2009)] and MapReduce [Chen *et al.* (2011)] workloads for Class-I and Class-II traffic. This setting coarsely models the workload for OLDI applications and distributed storage.

In our experiments, deadline-sensitive traffic uses D^2TCP [Vamanan *et al.* (2012b)], latency-sensitive uses DCTCP [Alizadeh *et al.* (2011)], and completion-sensitive traffic uses L^2DCT [Munir *et al.* (2013c)] transport protocol at the endhosts. We use default parameters, from respective chapters, for each of the protocol. The applications generate traffic according to a poisson process, such that the average bandwidth requirement of each class is 300 Mbps to meet its requirements. For deadline flows, the deadlines are exponentially distributed using guidelines from [Munir *et al.* (2013c)].

5.6   Comparison in Coexistence Scenario

In this section, we evaluate the impact of interference, on application performance, when flows with different performance objectives coexist in the network.

Coexistence Performance w/o In-Tunnel Algorithms: In this section, we show the benefits of using in-tunnel scheduling algorithms on top of objective-tunnel scheduling mechanism. To illustrate the benefits, we reuse

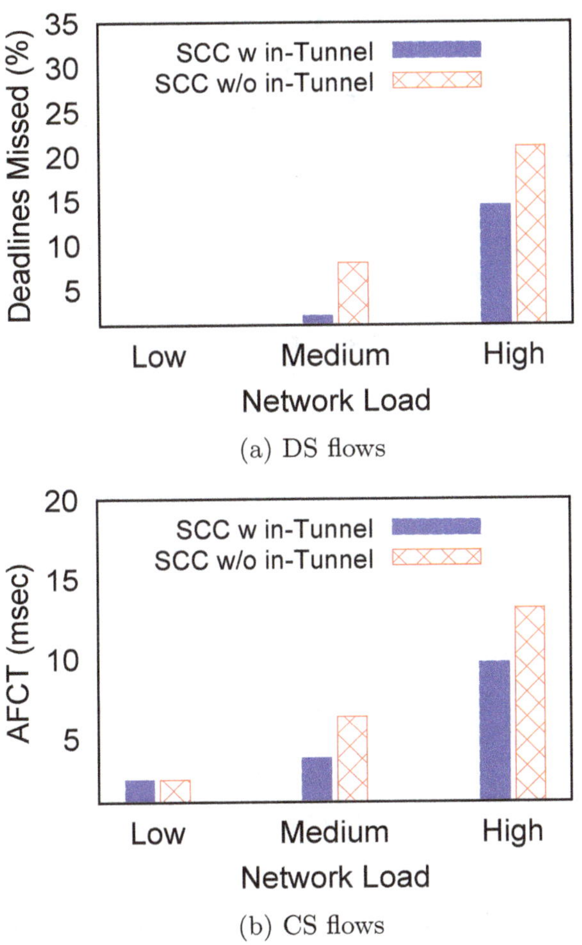

(a) DS flows

(b) CS flows

Fig. 5.4   Benefits of In-tunnel algorithm.

the simulation setup of motivation example and show the performance when DS and CS flows coexist in Fig. 5.4. As shown in Figure 5.4(a), the deadline miss ratio of DS flows reduces by up to 8% when in-tunnel scheduling is used. Similarly, as shown in Figure 5.4(b), the AFCT performance of CS flows reduces by up to 6% when in-tunnel scheduling is used. This shows that simple in-queue scheduling can further provide benefits on top of the tunnel level abstraction. We observe similar gains in other scenarios. In all other experiments, we use in-tunnel scheduling algorithms.

Coexist-LS/DS/CS Performance: In the first setup, we consider data-mining workload and assume that the flows of the three objectives (i.e.,

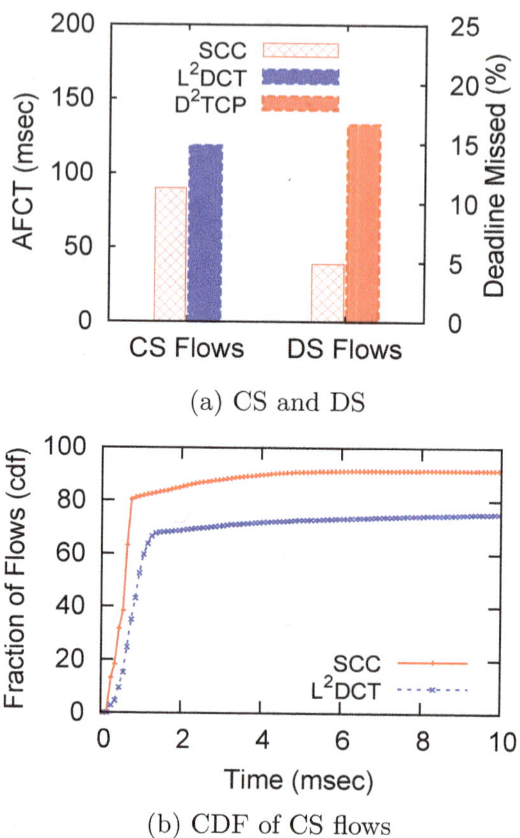

(a) CS and DS

(b) CDF of CS flows

Fig. 5.5   Coexistence of CS/DS/LS flows with datamining workload.

latency-sensitive, deadline-sensitive and completion-sensitive) coexist in the network. The aggregate workload generated by traffic from three objectives is 900 Mbps, generating 90% network load. Figure 5.5 shows that when the three objectives coexist without SCC support, they affect each other's performance. Data-mining workload is more skewed and more than 80% of the flows are less than 2 KB, SCC completes 3.2× more flows than without SCC, in Figure 5.5(a). SCC mitigates network interference and improves the AFCT by 40% compared to network without SCC support, in Figure 5.5(b). SCC, improves latency of latency-sensitive flows' by up to 40%. We omit results due to space limitation.

Coexistence performance of different objectives also hurts in the presence of interference traffic without SCC. To evaluate the impact of interference, we consider same settings as above and use Data-mining workload.

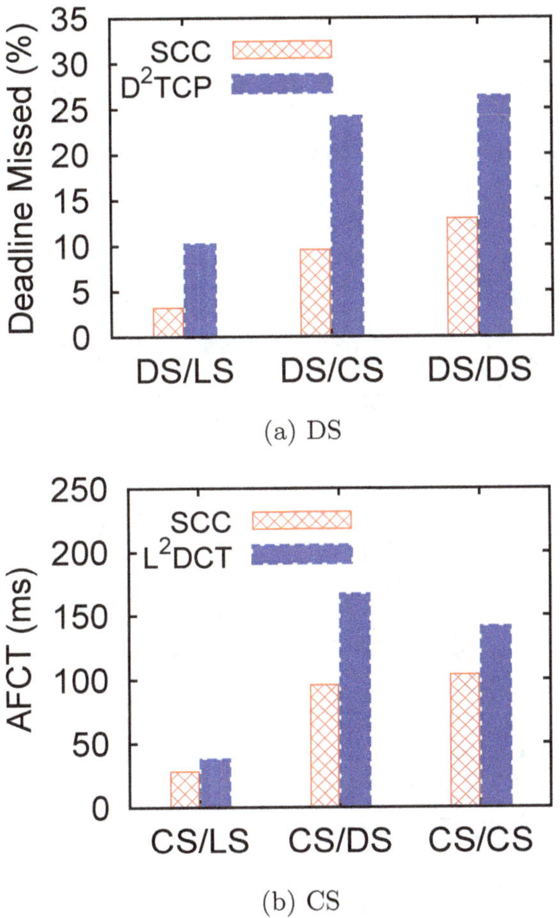

(a) DS

(b) CS

Fig. 5.6 Coexistence with Data-mining workload.

When coexisting, DS flows miss lots of deadlines because of interference in Figure 5.6(a). While coexistence with CS and LS flows, SCC reduces the deadline miss ratio by up to 3×. When coexisting, CS performance affects more in the presence of DS flows in the network, in Figure 5.6(b). However, when coexisting with only LS flows, the AFCT is not degraded. The reason is that there is sufficient capacity available in the network and flows do not experience queuing delays.

Comparison with State-of-the-Art: We also compare the SCC performance with state-of-the-art protocols such as pFabric [Alizadeh *et al.* (2013b)] that consider the coexistence of different objectives like CS/DS.

We consider coexistence of CS and DS flows using data-mining workload and each application generates 40% load in the network. For pFabric, we assign high priority to DS flows as compared to the CS flows. Figure 5.7(a) shows that SCC improves the performance of the CS flows by 30%, compared to pFabric. However, SCC misses 2% more deadlines for DS flows. This is expected as, in this scenario, SCC does not enforce any specific prioritization policy in the network.

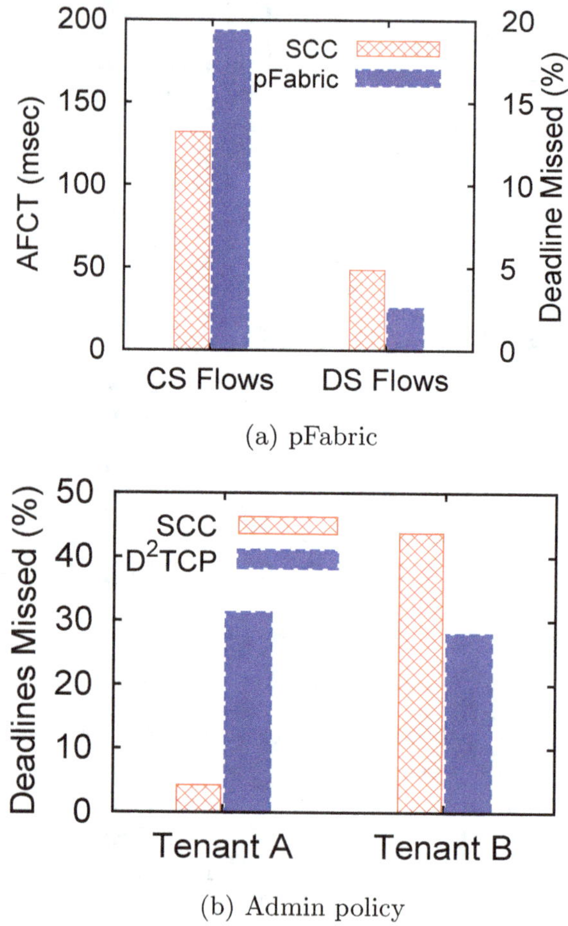

(a) pFabric

(b) Admin policy

Fig. 5.7   Comparison under Data-mining workload.

5.7 Comparison in Policy Enforcement

In this section, we consider the coexistence performance of same tenants or objectives but with constraints on the available network bandwidth and weight. We consider two tenants (A and B) with DS objective and both the tenants require 600 Mbps bandwidth to meet the deadline requirements of their applications. We assume that tenant A has more priority in the network, thus operator assigns more bandwidth to A and assigns rest of the available bandwidth to the tenant B. Figure 5.7(b) shows that SCC meets almost all the deadlines of Tenant A, however, the performance degrades for Tenant B. SCC meets more deadlines for both the Tenants combined.

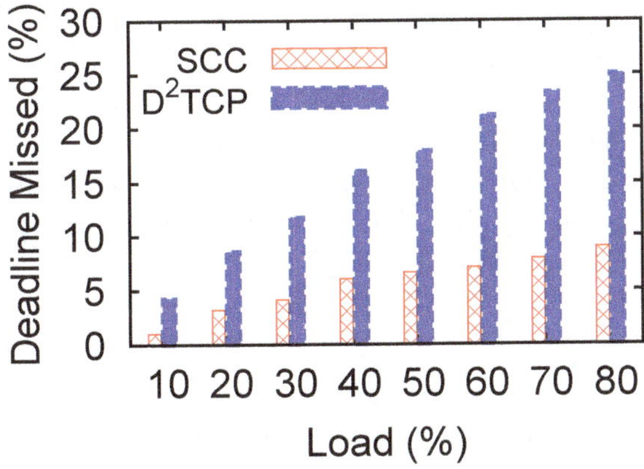

(a) DS flows' missed deadline

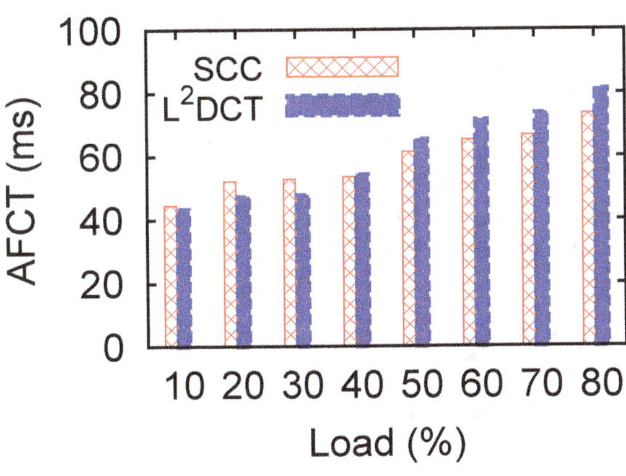

(b) CS flows' AFCT

Fig. 5.8   Isolation scenario.

5.8   Comparison in Isolation Scenario

In this setup, we evaluate performance of SCC for deadline-sensitive and completion-sensitive objectives when they have exclusive access to the network and compare it to the performance of D^2TCP and L^2DCT protocols respectively. The goal is to evaluate if, in the absence of coexistence, SCC can achieve similar performance as the transport protocols across a range of network loads. We use data-mining workload and use same network setup as in section 5.5.

For deadline-sensitive applications, SCC meets more deadlines across all the network loads and reduces the deadline missing by up to 2.5× (Figure 5.8(a)). This shows that SCC not only eliminates interference among flows of different objectives, but also improves performance via the abstraction of objective-tenant congestion-free tunnel.

For completion-sensitive applications, SCC minimizes the AFCT and achieves performance similar to L^2DCT, as shown in Figure 5.8(b). SCC achieves similar performance as L^2DCT at low loads and improves AFCT at higher loads by eliminating the inter-flow interference via its priority sub-queues.

5.9   SCC Dynamics

In this section, we evaluate SCC performance under different workloads, network oversubscription, different transport protocols, and strict priority. **Coexist-LS/DS/CS Performance under different workloads:** Next, we evaluate CS/DS/LS co-existence performance under different workloads in the network. The aggregate workload generated by traffic from three objectives is 900 Mbps, generating 90% network load.

Figure 5.9 shows that when the three objectives coexist without SCC support, they affect each other performance. SCC, reducers AFCT of CS flows' by up to 40%, 24%, 32% for Data-mining, Web-search, and MapReduce Figure 5.9(a). SCC reduces deadline missing ratio by 3.2×/1.8×/0.8× for the Data-mining, Web-search, and MapReduce workloads respectively, Figure 5.9(b). We observe similar trends for Web-search and MapReduce workloads.

Over-subscribed Network Scenario: We evaluate SCC on a 3:1 over-subscribed network. In this topology, we have 4 ToR switches, each connecters to 30 hosts with 1 Gbps links and connects to core switches using 10 Gbps links. We generate east-to-west traffic: all traffic is inter-rack.

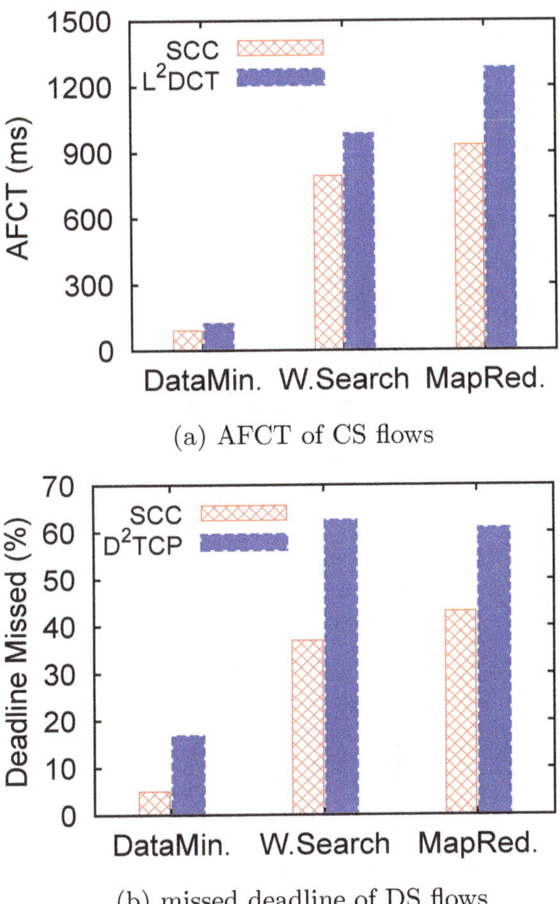

(a) AFCT of CS flows

(b) missed deadline of DS flows

Fig. 5.9 Coexistence with and without SCC support for different workloads.

Note that load is calculated based on network core load compared to previous scenarios, where the load was generated based on the edge links. We consider three applications, CS, DS and LS in the network. All the flows follow the Web-search workload and have average network load of 300 Mbps each. Figure 5.10(a) shows that SCC reduces AFCT of CS flows by 20% and reduces deadline missing ratio of DS traffic only marginally.

Different Transport Protocol: Figure 5.10(b) shows that even with DCTCP as transport protocol, SCC improves the application performance compared to the original protocols. The AFCT of CS flows improves by $3\times$ as these flows get equal share of the network bandwidth as DS flows.

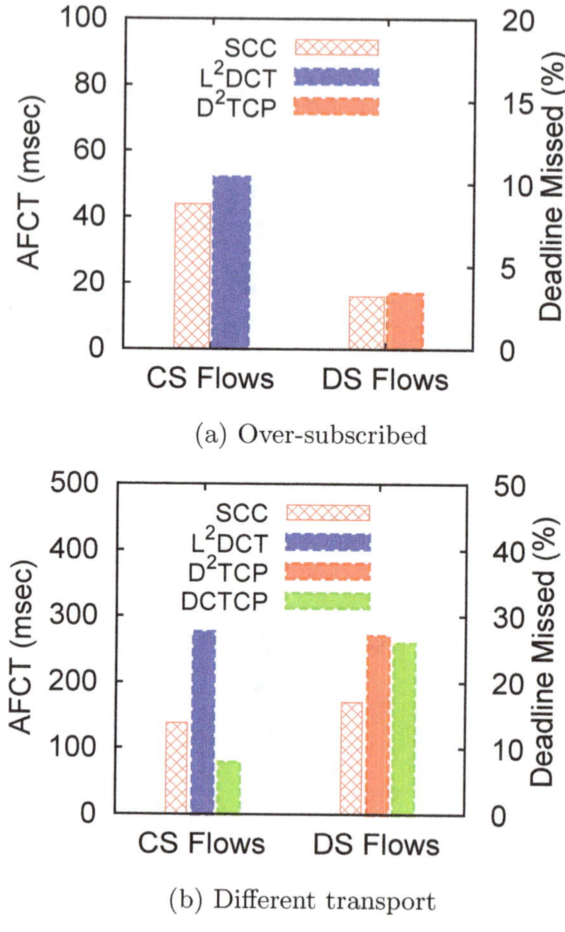

(a) Over-subscribed

(b) Different transport

Fig. 5.10   SCC Dynamics.

DCTCP is more aggressive in increasing rate than the L^2DCT, for large flows DCTCP increases congestion window by 1 pkt/RTT whereas L^2DCT increases by the factor k, where $k \in 0.5, 1$, which depends on the flow size. The performance of DS flows is also better than D^2TCP protocol, however, the deadline performance degrades compared to the scenario where SCC uses D^2TCP as the transport protocol. The reason is that now both CS and DS flows share network fairly and benefits of D^2TCP at the transport layer are lost.

Isolating Tenants using Priority Queues: In this section, we compare and contrast the tradeoffs of using priority queues inside the switches, to

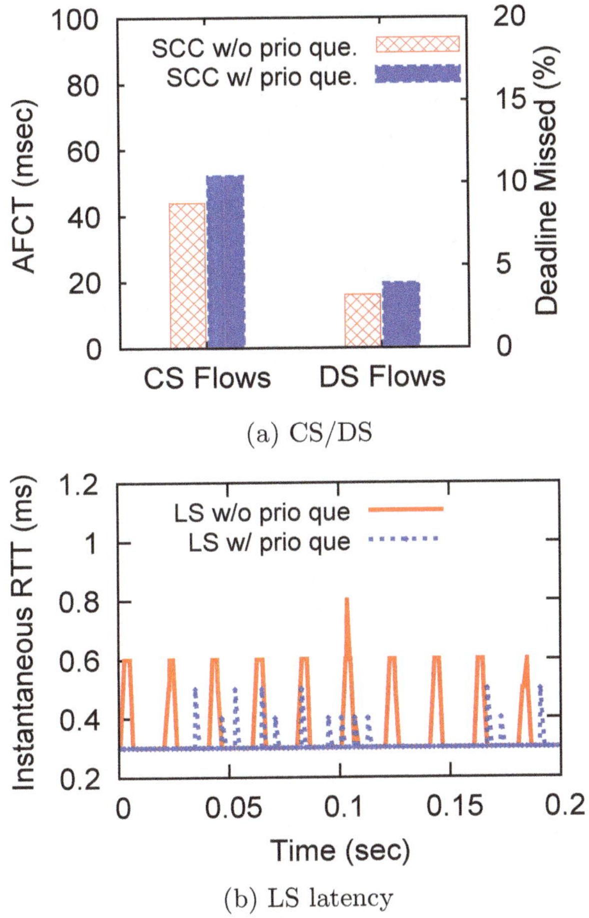

(a) CS/DS

(b) LS latency

Fig. 5.11   Objective isolation using priority queues.

isolate LS flows from other objectives to meet its requirements. To illustrate the benefits, we consider a network with two priority queues and coexistence of LS, DS and CS flows. Here, LS flows are mapped to the higher priority queue and CS/DS flows share the lower priority queue. Figure 5.11(a) shows that the performance of DS and CS flows is hurt a little when LS flows are prioritized over them. However, latency requirements of LS flows are better met when strict priority is enforced in switch queues, in Figure 5.11(b).

5.10   Conclusions

There exist two kinds of stakeholders in a datacenter networks: the tenants and the administrators. An individual tenant's congestion control tries to achieve its own performance objective. With a global view of the network, the administrators need to maximize its utility function. SCC provides a framework to decouple the congestion control among different performance objectives, from the congestion control among flows with the same objective. SCC demonstrates that simple solutions can be adopted to eliminate the interference among different performance objectives and different tenants.

Bibliography

(2006). Apache hadoop yarn, `https://goo.gl/qEdpo5`.

(2006). The network simulator - ns-2, `http://www.isi.edu/nsnam/ns/`.

(2006). Prio qdisc linux. `http://linux.die.net/man/8/tc-prio`.

(2014). Arista 7050s switch. `http://www.aristanetworks.com/docs/Manuals/ConfigGuide.pdf`.

(2014). Broadcom bcm56820 switch. `http://www.broadcom.com/collateral/pb/56820-PB00-R.pdf`.

(2014). Dell force10 s4810 switch. `http://www.force10networks.com/CSPortal20/KnowledgeBase/DOCUMENTATION/CLIConfig/FTOS/Z9000_CLI_8.3.11.4_23-May-2012.pdf`.

(2014). Ibm rackswitch g8264 application guide. `http://www.bladenetwork.net/userfiles/file/G8264_AG_6-8.pdf`.

(2014). Juniper ex3300 switch. `http://www.juniper.net/us/en/products-services/switching/ex-series/ex3300/`.

Abts, D. and Felderman, B. (2012). A guided tour of data-center networking, *Commun. ACM* **55**, 6, pp. 44–51.

Ahmad, F., Chakradhar, S. T., Raghunathan, A., and Vijaykumar, T. (2014). Shufflewatcher: Shuffle-aware scheduling in multi-tenant mapreduce clusters, in *USENIX ATC* (USENIX), pp. 1–12.

Al-Fares, M., Loukissas, A., and Vahdat, A. (2008). A scalable, commodity data center network architecture, in *ACM SIGCOMM Computer Communication Review*, Vol. 38 (ACM), pp. 63–74.

Al-Fares, M., Radhakrishnan, S., Raghavan, B., Huang, N., and Vahdat, A. (2010). Hedera: dynamic flow scheduling for data center networks, in *NSDI'10*.

Alizadeh, M., Greenberg, A., Maltz, D. A., Padhye, J., Patel, P., Prabhakar, B., Sengupta, S., and Sridharan, M. (2011). Data center tcp (dctcp), in *in Proc. ACM SIGCOMM 2011*, Vol. 41 (ACM), pp. 63–74.

Alizadeh, M., Greenberg, A. G., Maltz, D. A., Padhye, J., Patel, P., Prabhakar, B., Sengupta, S., and Sridharan, M. (2010). Data center TCP (DCTCP), in *SIGCOMM'10*, pp. 63–74.

Alizadeh, M., Kabbani, A., Edsall, T., Prabhakar, B., Vahdat, A., and Yasuda, M. (2012). Less is more: trading a little bandwidth for ultra-low latency in the data center, in *NSDI* (USENIX), pp. 19–19.

Alizadeh, M., Yang, S., Sharif, M., Katti, S., McKeown, N., Prabhakar, B., and Shenker, S. (2013a). pfabric: Minimal near-optimal datacenter transport, *ACM SIGCOMM Computer Communication Review* **43**, 4, pp. 435–446.

Alizadeh, M., Yang, S., Sharif, M., Katti, S., McKeown, N., Prabhakar, B., and Shenker, S. (2013b). pfabric: Minimal near-optimal datacenter transport, in *ACM SIGCOMM 2013*, Vol. 43 (ACM), pp. 435–446.

Ananthanarayanan, G., Ghodsi, A., Shenker, S., and Stoica, I. (2013). Effective straggler mitigation: Attack of the clones. in *NSDI*, Vol. 13 (USENIX), pp. 185–198.

Ananthanarayanan, G., Kandula, S., Greenberg, A. G., Stoica, I., Lu, Y., Saha, B., and Harris, E. (2010). Reining in the outliers in map-reduce clusters using mantri. in *OSDI*, Vol. 10, p. 24.

Bai, W., Chen, L., Chen, K., Han, D., Tian, C., and Wang, H. (2015). Information-agnostic flow scheduling for commodity data centers, in *NSDI* (USENIX).

Benson, T., Akella, A., and Maltz, D. A. (2010). Network traffic characteristics of data centers in the wild, in *ACM IMC* (ACM), pp. 267–280.

Borthakur, D. (2007). The hadoop distributed file system: Architecture and design, *Hadoop Project Website* **11**, 2007, p. 21.

Chang, H., Kodialam, M., Kompella, R. R., Lakshman, T., Lee, M., and Mukherjee, S. (2011). Scheduling in mapreduce-like systems for fast completion time, in *INFOCOM, 2011 Proceedings IEEE* (IEEE), pp. 3074–3082.

Chen, F., Kodialam, M., and Lakshman, T. (2012). Joint scheduling of processing and shuffle phases in mapreduce systems, in *INFOCOM, 2012 Proceedings IEEE* (IEEE), pp. 1143–1151.

Chen, L., Chen, K., Bai, W., and Alizadeh, M. (2016). scheduling mix-flows in commodity datacenters with karuna, in *ACM SIGCOMM, 2016*, Vol. 42 (ACM), pp. 1–12.

Chen, L., Hu, S., Chen, K., Wu, H., and Tsang, D. H. K. (2013). Towards minimal-delay deadline-driven data center tcp, in *Hotnets'13*.

Chen, Y., Ganapathi, A., Griffith, R., and Katz, R. (2011). The case for evaluating mapreduce performance using workload suites, in *IEEE MASCOTS'11* (IEEE), pp. 390–399.

Chowdhury, M., Kandula, S., and Stoica, I. (2013). Leveraging endpoint flexibility in data-intensive clusters, in *ACM SIGCOMM*, Vol. 43 (ACM), pp. 231–242.

Chowdhury, M. and Stoica, I. (2012). Coflow: a networking abstraction for cluster applications, in *ACM Hotnets* (ACM), pp. 31–36.

Chowdhury, M. and Stoica, I. (2015). Efficient coflow scheduling without prior knowledge, in *ACM SIGCOMM* (ACM), pp. 393–406.

Chowdhury, M., Zhong, Y., and Stoica, I. (2014). Efficient coflow scheduling with varys, in *ACM SIGCOMM* (ACM), pp. 443–454.

Costa, P., Donnelly, A., Rowstron, A., and O'Shea, G. (2012). Camdoop: exploiting in-network aggregation for big data applications, in *Proceedings of the 9th USENIX conference on Networked Systems Design and Implementation* (USENIX Association), pp. 3–3.

Curtis, A., Mogul, J., Tourrilhes, J., Yalagandula, P., Sharma, P., and Banerjee, S. (2011). Devoflow: scaling flow management for high-performance networks, in *SIGCOMM'11*.

Dean, J. and Barroso, L. A. (2013). The tail at scale, *Communications of the ACM, 2013* **56**, 2, pp. 74–80.

Dean, J. and Ghemawat, S. (2004). MapReduce: Simplified Data Processing on Large Clusters, in *OSDI'04*.

Dean, J. and Ghemawat, S. (2008). Mapreduce: simplified data processing on large clusters, *Communications of the ACM* **51**, 1, pp. 107–113.

DeCandia, G., Hastorun, D., Jampani, M., Kakulapati, G., Lakshman, A., Pilchin, A., Sivasubramanian, S., Vosshall, P., and Vogels, W. (2007). Dynamo: amazon's highly available key-value store, in *in ACM SIGOPS 2007*, Vol. 41 (ACM), pp. 205–220.

Dogar, F. R., Karagiannis, T., Ballani, H., and Rowstron, A. (2014a). Decentralized task-aware scheduling for data center networks, in *ACM SIGCOMM* (ACM), pp. 431–442.

Dogar, F. R., Karagiannis, T., Ballani, H., and Rowstron, A. (2014b). Decentralized Task-aware Scheduling for Data Center Networks, in *SIGCOMM'14*.

Engle, C., Lupher, A., Xin, R., Zaharia, M., Franklin, M. J., Shenker, S., and Stoica, I. (2012). Shark: fast data analysis using coarse-grained distributed memory, in *ACM SIGMOD 2012* (ACM), pp. 689–692.

Farrington, N. and Andreyev, A. (2013). Facebook data center network architecture, in *IEEE Optical Interconnects Conf* (Citeseer).

Gao, P. X., Narayan, A., Kumar, G., Agarwal, R., Ratnasamy, S., and Shenker, S. (2015). phost: Distributed near-optimal datacenter transport over commodity network fabric, in *Proceedings of the CoNEXT*.

Ghodsi, A., Sekar, V., Zaharia, M., and Stoica, I. (2012). Multi-resource fair queueing for packet processing, in *ACM SIGCOMM*, Vol. 42 (ACM), pp. 1–12.

Ghodsi, A., Zaharia, M., Hindman, B., Konwinski, A., Shenker, S., and Stoica, I. (2011). Dominant resource fairness: Fair allocation of multiple resource types. in *NSDI*, Vol. 11 (USENIX), pp. 24–24.

Ghodsi, A., Zaharia, M., Shenker, S., and Stoica, I. (2013). Choosy: Max-min fair sharing for datacenter jobs with constraints, in *ACM EuroSys* (ACM), pp. 365–378.

Greenberg, A., Hamilton, J. R., Jain, N., Kandula, S., Kim, C., Lahiri, P., Maltz, D. A., Patel, P., and Sengupta, S. (2009). Vl2: a scalable and flexible data center network, in *ACM SIGCOMM 2009*, Vol. 39 (ACM), pp. 51–62.

Gropp, W., Huss-Lederman, S., Lumsdaine, A., Lusk, E., Nitzberg, B., Saphir, W., and Snir, M. (1998). Mpi, *The Complete Reference. The MPI-2 Extensions* **2**.

Grosvenor, M. P., Schwarzkopf, M., Gog, I., Watson, R. N., Moore, A. W., Hand,

S., and Crowcroft, J. (2015). Queues don't matter when you can jump them! in *NSDI* (USENIX).

Guo, C., Lu, G., Wang, H. J., Yang, S., Kong, C., Sun, P., Wu, W., and Zhang, Y. (2010). Secondnet: a data center network virtualization architecture with bandwidth guarantees, in *ACM CoNext 2010* (ACM), p. 15.

He, K., Rozner, E., Agarwal, K., Felter, W., Carter, J., and Akella, A. (2015). Presto: Edge-based load balancing for fast datacenter networks, *ACM SIG-COMM Computer Communication Review, 2015* **45**, 4, pp. 465–478.

Hindman, B., Konwinski, A., Zaharia, M., Ghodsi, A., Joseph, A. D., Katz, R. H., Shenker, S., and Stoica, I. (2011). Mesos: A platform for fine-grained resource sharing in the data center. in *NSDI*, Vol. 11 (USENIX), pp. 22–22.

Hong, C., Caesar, M., and Godfrey, P. (2012a). Finishing flows quickly with preemptive scheduling, in *SIGCOMM'12*.

Hong, C.-Y., Caesar, M., and Godfrey, P. (2012b). Finishing flows quickly with preemptive scheduling, in *Proc. ACM SIGCOMM 2012*, Vol. 42 (ACM), pp. 127–138.

Hu, S., Bai, W., Chen, K., Tian, C., Zhang, Y., and Wu, H. (2016). Providing bandwidth guarantees, work conservation and low latency simultaneously in the cloud, in *Proceedings of infocom*.

Isard, M., Budiu, M., Yu, Y., Birrell, A., and Fetterly, D. (2007). Dryad: distributed data-parallel programs from sequential building blocks, in *ACM SIGOPS Operating Systems Review*, Vol. 41 (ACM), pp. 59–72.

Isard, M., Prabhakaran, V., Currey, J., Wieder, U., Talwar, K., and Goldberg, A. (2009). Quincy: fair scheduling for distributed computing clusters, in *ACM SIGOPS* (ACM), pp. 261–276.

Jalaparti, V., Bodik, P., Kandula, S., Menache, I., Rybalkin, M., and Yan, C. (2013). Speeding up distributed request-response workflows, in *ACM SIG-COMM 2013*, Vol. 43 (ACM), pp. 219–230.

Jalaparti, V., Bodik, P., Menache, I., Rao, S., Makarychev, K., and Caesar, M. (2015). Network-aware scheduling for data-parallel jobs: Plan when you can, in *ACM SIGCOMM* (ACM), pp. 407–420.

Jang, K., Sherry, J., Ballani, H., and Moncaster, T. (2015). Silo: Predictable message latency in the cloud, in *in Proc. ACM SIGDC, 2015* (ACM), pp. 435–448.

Jeyakumar, V., Alizadeh, M., Mazieres, D., Prabhakar, B., Kim, C., and Greenberg, A. (2013a). Eyeq: practical network performance isolation at the edge, in *NSDI* (USENIX).

Jeyakumar, V., Alizadeh, M., Mazieres, D., Prabhakar, B., Kim, C., and Greenberg, A. (2013b). EyeQ: Practical Network Performance Isolation at the Edge, in *NSDI'13*.

Judd, G. (2015). Attaining the promise and avoiding the pitfalls of tcp in the datacenter, in *12th USENIX Symposium on Networked Systems Design and Implementation (NSDI 15)*, pp. 145–157.

Katabi, D., Handley, M., and Rohrs, C. (2002). Congestion Control for High Bandwidth-Delay Product Networks, in *SIGCOMM*.

Kumar, G., Kandula, S., Bodik, P., and Menache, I. (2013). Virtualizing traffic shapers for practical resource allocation, in *HotCloud'13*.

Lee, J., Turner, Y., Lee, M., Popa, L., Banerjee, S., Kang, J.-M., and Sharma, P. (2014). Application-driven bandwidth guarantees in datacenters, in *ACM SIGCOMM* (ACM), pp. 467–478.

Malewicz, G., Austern, M. H., Bik, A. J., Dehnert, J. C., Horn, I., Leiser, N., and Czajkowski, G. (2010). Pregel: a system for large-scale graph processing, in *ACM SIGMOD 2010*, pp. 135–146.

Melnik, S., Gubarev, A., Long, J. J., Romer, G., Shivakumar, S., Tolton, M., and Vassilakis, T. (2010). Dremel: interactive analysis of web-scale datasets, *in Proc. of the VLDB 2010* **3**, 1-2, pp. 330–339.

Mittal, R., Dukkipati, N., Blem, E., Wassel, H., Ghobadi, M., Vahdat, A., Wang, Y., Wetherall, D., Zats, D., *et al.* (2015). Timely: Rtt-based congestion control for the datacenter, in *Proc. ACM SIGDC 2015* (ACM), pp. 537–550.

Munir, A., Baig, G., Irteza, S. M., Qazi, I. A., Liu, A. X., and Dogar, F. R. (2014). Friends, not foes: synthesizing existing transport strategies for data center networks, in *ACM SIGCOMM 2014* (ACM), pp. 491–502.

Munir, A., Qazi, I. A., and Bin Qaisar, S. (2013a). On achieving low latency in data centers, in *ICC* (IEEE), pp. 3721–3725.

Munir, A., Qazi, I. A., Uzmi, Z. A., Mushtaq, A., Ismail, S. N., Iqbal, M. S., and Khan, B. (2013b). Minimizing Flow Completion Times in Data Centers, in *INFOCOM'13*.

Munir, A., Qazi, I. A., Uzmi, Z. A., Mushtaq, A., Ismail, S. N., Iqbal, M. S., and Khan, B. (2013c). Minimizing flow completion times in data centers, in *in Proc. IEEE INFOCOM, 2013* (IEEE), pp. 2157–2165.

Nishtala, R., Fugal, H., Grimm, S., Kwiatkowski, M., Lee, H., Li, H. C., McElroy, R., Paleczny, M., Peek, D., Saab, P., Stafford, D., Tung, T., and Venkataramani, V. (2013). Scaling memcache at facebook, in *NSDI'13*.

Perry, J., Ousterhout, A., Balakrishnan, H., Shah, D., and Fugal, H. (2014). Fastpass: A centralized zero-queue datacenter network, in *ACM SIGCOMM* (ACM), pp. 307–318.

Popa, L., Kumar, G., Chowdhury, M., Krishnamurthy, A., Ratnasamy, S., and Stoica, I. (2012). Faircloud: sharing the network in cloud computing, in *ACM SIGCOMM 2012* (ACM), pp. 187–198.

Popa, L., Yalagandula, P., Banerjee, S., Mogul, J. C., Turner, Y., and Santos, J. R. (2013). Elasticswitch: practical work-conserving bandwidth guarantees for cloud computing, in *ACM SIGCOMM 2013*, Vol. 43 (ACM), pp. 351–362.

Ren, X., Ananthanarayanan, G., Wierman, A., and Yu, M. (2015). Hopper: Decentralized speculation-aware cluster scheduling at scale, in *ACM SIG-COMM* (ACM), pp. 379–392.

Rodrigues, H., Santos, J. R., Turner, Y., Soares, P., and Guedes, D. (2011). Gatekeeper: Supporting bandwidth guarantees for multi-tenant datacenter networks, in *WIOV*.

Shieh, A., Kandula, S., Greenberg, A. G., Kim, C., and Saha, B. (2011). Sharing the data center network, in *NSDI*.

Singh, A., Ong, J., Agarwal, A., Anderson, G., Armistead, A., Bannon, R., Boving, S., Desai, G., Felderman, B., Germano, P., *et al.* (2015). Jupiter rising: A decade of clos topologies and centralized control in google's datacenter network, in *Proc. ACM SIGDC 2015* (ACM), pp. 183–197.

Sivaraman, A., Winstein, K., Subramanian, S., and Balakrishnan, H. (2013). No silver bullet: extending sdn to the data plane, in *Proceedings of the Twelfth ACM Workshop on Hot Topics in Networks* (ACM), p. 19.

Tan, J., Chin, A., Hu, Z. Z., Hu, Y., Meng, S., Meng, X., and Zhang, L. (2014). Dynmr: Dynamic mapreduce with reduce task interleaving and maptask backfilling, in *ACM EuroSys* (ACM), p. 2.

Vamanan, B., Hasan, J., and Vijaykumar, T. (2012a). Deadline-aware datacenter tcp (d^2tcp), in *SIGCOMM'12*.

Vamanan, B., Hasan, J., and Vijaykumar, T. (2012b). Deadline-aware datacenter tcp (d2tcp), in *ACM SIGCOMM* (ACM), pp. 115–126.

Vavilapalli, V. K., Murthy, A. C., Douglas, C., Agarwal, S., Konar, M., Evans, R., Graves, T., Lowe, J., Shah, H., Seth, S., *et al.* (2013). Apache hadoop yarn: Yet another resource negotiator, in *ACM SoCC* (ACM), p. 5.

Wilson, C., Ballani, H., Karagiannis, T., and Rowstron, A. (2011a). Better never than late: Meeting deadlines in datacenter networks, in *SIGCOMM'11*.

Wilson, C., Ballani, H., Karagiannis, T., and Rowtron, A. (2011b). Better never than late: Meeting deadlines in datacenter networks, in *ACM SIGCOMM* (ACM), pp. 50–61.

Zaharia, M., Borthakur, D., Sen Sarma, J., Elmeleegy, K., Shenker, S., and Stoica, I. (2010). Delay scheduling: a simple technique for achieving locality and fairness in cluster scheduling, in *ACM EuroSys* (ACM), pp. 265–278.

Zaharia, M., Konwinski, A., Joseph, A. D., Katz, R. H., and Stoica, I. (2008). Improving mapreduce performance in heterogeneous environments. in *OSDI*, Vol. 8, p. 7.

Zats, D., Das, T., Mohan, P., Borthakur, D., and Katz, R. (2012a). Detail: reducing the flow completion time tail in datacenter networks, in *ACM SIGCOMM*, Vol. 42 (ACM), pp. 139–150.

Zats, D., Das, T., Mohan, P., Borthakur, D., and Katz, R. (2012b). Detail: Reducing the flow completion time tail in datacenter networks, in *SIGCOMM'12*.

Zhang, H., Chen, K., Bai, W., Han, D., Tian, C., Wang, H., Guan, H., and Zhang, M. (2015). Guaranteeing deadlines for inter-datacenter transfers, in *Proceedings of the Tenth European Conference on Computer Systems* (ACM), p. 20.

Zhao, Y., Chen, K., Bai, W., Tian, C., Geng, Y., Zhang, Y., Li, D., and Wang, S. (2015). Rapier: Integrating routing and scheduling for coflow-aware data center networks, in *Proc. IEEE INFOCOM*.

Index